D1871111

An Introduction to Comparative Government and Politics

An Introduction to Comparative Government and Politics

As Per the Syllabus of Assam University and Bodoland University

B.A Third Semester (Major)

Jesmine Ahmed

©Author

All rights reserved. No part of this work may be reproduced, stored, adapted, or transmitted in any form or by any means, electronic, mechanical, photocopying, micro-filming recording or otherwise, or translated in any language, without the prior written permission of the copyright owner and the publisher. The book is sold subject to the condition that it shall not, by way of trade or otherwise, be lent, resold, hired out, or otherwise circulated without the prior publisher's written consent in any form of binding or cover other than that in which it is published.

The views and opinions expressed in this book are author(s) own and the facts reported by them have been verified to the extent possible, and the publishers are not in any way liable for the same.

ISBN: 978-93-5324-296-1

First Published, 2020

Published by

Kalpaz Publications
C-30, Satyawati Nagar,
Delhi – 110052
Ph.: 011-47034999, 9811692060
www.kalpazpublications.com
E-mail: kalpaz@hotmail.com

Printed at: G. Print Process, Delhi

Contents

Preface

The idea of writing this book came out with a purpose of provide holistic knowledge about the respective subject. It tries to give a brief knowledge about Comparative Government and Politics and its related issues. Since politics and government is very relevant topic that illustrates the diverse governments across the world, it does help to study political life, constitutional development and alternative governments along with their changing political economy. It also deals with the historical context of modern government.

Further, the content of the present book focuses on four core countries including China, Great Britain, Brazil and Nigeria. By studying the four vastly different political structures, learner can get a full understanding of the diversity of political systems across the globe.

So with this I try to make this book resourceful and hope this effort would able to create a sense of understanding among the readers of Compartaive Government and Politcs.

Jesmine Ahmed
M.A, NET, M.Phil.

Acknowledgement

I express my pleasure in presenting my book Comparative Government and Politics before its readers. This book is written in accordance with the new syllabus of U.G.C and several universities throughout India. This book provides its readers a better understanding of the subject in a simple and systematic manner.

I owe a debt of gratitude to various Indian and foreign authors whose standard texts I have consulted to incorporate each aspect that may prove helpful for the readers.

I would also like to pay my silence thanks to all those people who helped me in preparation of the book and, in particular, the publisher for taking personal interest and providing maximum possible co-operation.

I request the readers to feel free to provide their suggestions for improvement in the book. I sincerely hope that the book shall meet the expectations of the readers.

Jesmine Ahmed

M.A, NET, M.Phil.

Unit - I

Understanding Comparative Politics: Nature and Scope

Chapter - 1

Meaning, Nature and Scope of Comparative Politics

What is Comparative Politics?

There often arises a question regarding the clear meaning of Comparative Politics. Many textbooks on comparative politics give a simple answer to the question. The simplest one is that it is the comparative study of politics in different countries. But there are some formal meaning of the term that involves both a method of study and a subject of study[1]. As a method of study, it involves comparisons whereas as a subject of study, comparative politics concentrations on understanding and explaining political phenomenon that occurs within a state, society, country or political system. It provides a systematic, coherent and practical way to know and make better sense of the effects that happen in the world around us. Comparative politics pursuits for those similarities and differences between more than one nation-state that helps to explain the basic nature, working and belief of regimes. It concerned about the field that focuses on internal or domestic dynamics that helps to differentiate comparative politics from international relations-mostly stress on external relations or foreign policies of states. Moreover, it not only characterised but also defined by a comparative method of analysis.

Comparative Politics has a long-lasting history dating back to the very origin of systematic political studies in ancient Greece and Rome.

It involves the systematic study and comparison of the world political system. It seeks to explain differences as well as similarities among countries. Comparative Politics are particularly interested in exploring patterns, process and regularities among political systems.

According to E.A. Freeman, "Comparative Politics is a comparative analysis of the various forms of Government and diverse political institutions".

According to John Blondel, comparative politics is "the study of patterns of national governments in the contemporary world".

According to M.G. Smith, "Comparative politics is the study of the forms of political organisations, their properties, correlations, variations and modes of change."

Arend Lijphart argues that comparative politics does not have a substantive focus in itself, but rather a methodological one: it focuses on "the how but does not specify what of the analysis.[2]"

Peter Mair and Richard Rose defined that "Comparative politics is defined by a combination of a substantive focus on the study of countries political systems and a method of identifying and explaining similarities and differences between these countries using common concepts." Rose further stated that "the focus is explicitly or implicitly upon more than one country, thus following familiar political science usage in excluding within-nation comparison. Methodologically, a comparison is distinguished by its use of concepts that are applicable in more than one country.[3]"

According to M. Curtis, "Comparative Politics is concerned with significant regularities, similarities and differences in the working of political institutions and political behaviour.[4]"

According to Braibante, "Comparative politics is identification and interpretation of factors in the whole social order which appear to affect whatever political functions and their institutions which have been identified and listed for comparison.[5]"

Harry Eckstein has rightly observed that "Comparative Politics has a particular right to claim Aristotle as an ancestor because of the primacy he assigned to politics among the sciences and because the problems he raised and the methods he used are similar to those still current in political studies.[6]"

Based on all these definitions, it is evident that comparative politics involves a comparative study of not only the institutional arrangements but also an empirical and scientific analysis of non-institutionalised and non-political determinants of political behaviour.

Thus, comparative politics is necessary for a proper understanding of both international relations and foreign policy. As without an intimate knowledge of other countries with the help of which we usually conduct foreign relations, we cannot have an informed successful foreign policy at all.

Nature of Comparative Politics

The nature of Comparative Politics is understandable only when one can know about the nature and characteristics of Comparative Government. Though both the term often used interchangeably, there is a difference between the two. Comparative government is narrow than comparative politics. It includes the study of features and legal powers of political institutions existing in various states. It is the study of state and other political institutions in terms of their legal powers, functions, and positions on a comparative basis[7].

Some of the basic features of Comparative Government are: It emphasises on the study of the political institutions of different countries and their powers & functions accordingly; stress on the description of the features of the major constitutions of the world; formal study of various organisations and powers. These form the basis of comparative government study and it makes comparative government widespread area of study during the early 20th century. But most of the political scientists heavily dissatisfied with its narrower scope, normative and institutional nature and instinctive methodology. They then agree for comprehensiveness, precision and scientific study of the processes of politics as their new goal. It led to the emerging concept of Comparative Politics. Thus, Comparative Politics is all-encompassing in nature. Comparative political scientists assure that their studies include everything political[8].

The study of comparative politics comprises careful comparisons in studying political experiences, institutions, behaviour and processes of major systems of government. It comprises of the study of even extra-constitutional agencies along with the study of formal governmental organs. It is concerned with important regularities, similarities and differences in the working of political behaviour. Subsequently, Comparative Politics can be defined as the subject that compares the political systems in various parts of the world, with a vision to understand and explain the nature of politics and to formulate a scientific theory of politics.

Comparative Politics seeks to analyse and compare the political systems operating in various societies. It takes into account all the three characteristics of politics- political activity, the political process and political power.

Political Activity consists of all the activities involved in conflict resolution or the struggle for power. However, politics stands for the political process. It involves the study of all formal as well as non-formal structures through which the political process gets operationalized.

The political process receives information and signals from the environment and then transforms this information into authoritative values.

At last, politics being a struggle for power or a process of conflict resolution through the use of legitimate powers that involves the wide study of power or power relations in society. Lasswell describes politics as the process of shaping and sharing of power. However, Robert Dahl argues that politics contains the power to rule and authority to a significant extent.

Hence, the study of politics automatically comprises the study of power. As such comparative politics involves the study and comparison of political activity, the political process and struggle for power in the various political system in a brought way as well as through a comparative analysis of their structures, functions, infrastructures and processes.

Comparative politics rests on a variety of features. It holds analytical and Imperial research that is considered a value-free empirical study that rejects normative (value-laden), descriptive methods of comparative government. Moreover, this subject also studies the infrastructure of politics. As nowadays comparative politics explore the actual behaviour of individuals, groups, structures, subsystems and systems concerning its environment.

Comparative politics is an inter-disciplinary approach that study politics with the help of other social sciences like –psychology, sociology, and economics.

Scope

Comparative politics is a key area of political science. Its scope includes enhancing the ongoing condition of any nation. Initially, comparative politics confined itself with the study of governments and regime kinds of western countries. But after the Second World War when decolonisation process started, its scope embraces to the study of newly independent countries and brought a new range of comparisons. It required the need to formulate abstract-universal models that could help to study the political phenomenon in all divisions. More diversified studies were conducted in the scope of politics for enquiry of politics as a total system that includes not merely the state and its institutions but also individuals, social groupings, political parties, interest groups, social movements etc.

All Political Structures

The scope of Comparative Politics includes the study of all the formal and informal, governmental and extra-governmental, which are directly or indirectly involved in the struggle for power taking place in each state. It is not confined only to the study of the three formal governmental organs-legislature, executive and judiciary. Along with these, Bureaucracy, Interest Groups, Pressure Groups, Elites, Political Parties and all other political groups of human beings form a part of the scope of Comparative Politics.

Functional Studies

Comparative Politics seeks to study politics less from the legal institutions in terms of their powers, and more from the functions which constitute the political process and their actual operation in the environment. It studies the functions of interest articulation, interest aggregation, political communication, rule-making, rule-application, rule-adjudication, socialization, decision -making, policy-making and the like.

Study of Political Behaviour

Another important part of the scope of Comparative Politics is the study of the actual behaviour of the people in the process of politics. Voting behaviour, political participation, leadership recruitment, elite behaviour, mass politics, populism etc. form an integral part of Comparative Politics.

Study of Similarities and Differences

Comparative Politics also undertakes an analysis of the similarities and differences among political processes and functions. However, the approach is not descriptive, legalistic and formalistic. It is based on the actual functioning of political structures and processes that the similarities and dissimilarities are empirically explained, analyzed and compared. The objective is not to decide which is the best process or system. The objective is a systematic explanation, understanding, and theory- building.

Study of all Political Systems

Comparative Politics seeks to analyse the actual behaviour and performance of political systems-Western as well as non-Western. Political Systems are analysed and compared in terms of their structures, functions, capabilities and performances. Here again, the objective is not to decide which political system is the best. The actual working of various political systems is analysed to gather systematic knowledge for theory-building.

Study of the Environment and Infrastructure of Politics

The study of Politics demands a study of the psychological, sociological, economic and anthropological environment, in fact, the social environment as a whole, in which each political system operates. For studying this, modern political scientists have developed concepts like political culture, political socialization, political modernisation etc.

The study of the political culture of various political systems forms a very popular focus in comparative politics. Study of the Infrastructure of politics forms an integral part of the scope of Comparative Politics. This concept has enhanced the ability of political scientists to explain and compare the behaviour of various political systems in their environments. It has further helped them to analyse the differences in the working of similar political systems and the gaps between micro-politics and macro-politics.

Study of Political Culture

Political Culture is composed of attitudes, beliefs, emotions and values of a society that relate to the political system and political issues. These beliefs and values greatly influence the functioning of each political system. The study of Political Culture is an important part of the scope of Comparative Politics. Political Culture constitutes the psychological environment of each political system and hence deserves full attention.

Study of Political Socialisation

Political Socialisation is the process by which an individual acquires his Political Culture. It is also included in the scope of comparative politics because the behaviour of each political system depends to a large extent on this process. It is the process by which Political Cultures are maintained and changed.

Study of Political Participation

Political participation is a universal fact. The only difference is that in some states, it is limited while in others it is wider. Political participation provides legitimacy to the government and administration and brings stability in it because a system which is based on the consent and will of the people and where the participation of the people is wider, always more efficient and stable. The students of comparative politics seek to know how political participation influences the functional aspect of political systems in different states. Moreover, they also try to know the factors which determine political participation and their role in politics.

Study of Pressure Groups and Interest Groups

Organised groups are found in every political system. Some of them are formed voluntarily by individuals for fulfilling some special and common objectives e.g., Political Parties, Interest Groups and Pressure Groups, etc.

Besides, there are some groups which come into existence suddenly due to a particular event and remain in existence for a short period. These groups reflect the wishes of the people through public meetings, symbols, programmes, demonstrations, etc., and try to influence the working of the political system. Political Parties contest elections, form government, criticize the government and perform other such function.

There is a one-party system in communist countries (China); there are at work two-party systems in countries like the USA and the UK and some countries like India, France and Switzerland there are at work multi-party systems. The nature of the party systems and the number and activities of interest groups always exercise a deterministic role in the working of a democratic political system.

Therefore, the students of Comparative Politics have to evaluate minutely the structure, working and policy-programmes of these groups.

Study of Power, Influence, Authority and Legitimacy

Modern political scientists lay special emphasis on the study of 'Power.' 'Influence', 'Authority' and Legitimacy. They use these concepts for the classification of political systems based on the nature of authority relations and struggle for power. As such, the study of the concepts of Power, Influence, Legitimacy and Authority occupies an important place in the scope of Comparative Politics.

Study of Political Processes

Political processes like Decision-making, Policy-making, Judicial Process, Leadership recruitment process and others, are always at work in all political systems. The actual working of a political system depends upon these processes. Therefore, a comparative study of all the political processes is also an integral part of the scope of Comparative Politics.

Thus, the scope of Comparative Politics has become very comprehensive. It includes everything that falls within the purview of political activity and political process. It seeks to study all mechanisms of politics to build a science of politics capable of explaining and comparing all political activities, processes, and systems.

It involves a study of all structures and functions, which directly or indirectly, vigorously or passively affect the political processes in all states. Political Behaviour, Political Culture, Political Socialisation, Decision-making, Power-struggle, Interest Groups, Political Parties, Elites, Direct Action, Public Protests, Violence, Urbanisation, Modernisation, Power influence authority etc., are all included in the scope of Comparative Politics.

Evolution of Comparative Politics

Comparative Politics has been a very popular and useful subject of study within the broad ambit of Political Science. The study of Comparative politics dates back by the studies done by the Greek philosopher Aristotle. Aristotle studied the constitutions of 150 states and classified them into a typology of governments. His category was based on both descriptive and normative concern. Moreover, Aristotle analyses political systems in terms of e.g., democracy, aristocracy, monarchy etc. and he also distinguished them based on certain norms of good governance. On the basis of this comparison government divided into good and bad or ideal and perverted form.

Aristotelian categories were recognised and followed by Romans who considered them in formal and legalistic terms. This comparative study reappeared in the 15th century with Machiavelli (1469- 1527). After Aristotle, several political thinkers—Cicero, Polybius, Machiavelli, Montesquieu, J.S. Mill, Bagehot and others, used the comparative method in a highly productive way[9].

In the 19th century, Comparative Politics studies (Popularly designated as Comparative Government) were used by the political scientists for arriving at correct and valid conclusions regarding the nature and organisation of state and government through a comparative study of organisation, powers and functions of various political institutions working in various states. In the early 19th century comparative normative-prescriptive study of political institutions was conducted for answering these questions. The features, merits, demerits, similarities and dissimilarities of political institutions were compared and an attempt was made to identify the best political institutions. This focus continued to remain popular up till the late of the 19th century.

However, in the late 19th century and early 20th century, the ideology of liberalism got dominance in world politics. At that time comparative studies were dominated by the writings of James Bryce's 'Modern Democracies'(1921)'; 'Theory and Practice of Modern Governments (1932) by Herbert Finer; Carl J. Friedrich's (1932) 'Constitutional Government and Democracy' (1937), Roberto Michaels's 'Political Parties' (1915) and M. Duverger's Political Parties (1950) etc. Those studies largely concerned with the comparative study of institutions, the distribution of power, and the relationship between the different layers of government. These studies were concentrated purely on European countries like the British, France, Germany etc. It was not comparative in a true sense as most of the nations are excluded from comparing. Thus, in this period manifests the roots in the normative values of the western liberal democracies with emphasis on civilizational superiority.

Gradually socialism took its root at its peak with the Bolshevik Revolution in 1917 that was alternative to western liberalism and capitalism. However, in the 1930s the political and economic situation of the world changed and with the end of the Second World War, several major developments occurred such as weakening of British supremacy, the emergence of USA as the new superpower or hegemon in world politics & economy. Moreover, the division of the world into two ideological groups- one is 'Capitalism' and another is 'Socialism' followed by western and eastern countries respectively.

Apart from this, after the Second World War decolonisation process started and many European colonies emerged as independent countries. At this time, the concept of development, modernisation, state-building, nation-building got prominent. The newly independent nation, however, did not compel to follow the path of capitalism; as socialism was adopted by many emerging countries of Asia, Africa and Latin America, as well as some other countries by making a consensus, decided to keep themselves away from the power blocs and followed 'Non-Alignment'. Several countries adopted mixed-economy model (a combination of both capitalism and socialism).

In this way, comparative study confined to the study of institutions 1940s, but in the mid-1950s tremendous criticism arose against institutional approach. This criticism deeply influenced by behavioural revolution, an emerging movement that treated politics as a science of politics. This movement rejects values and based on the examination of empirical facts, quantitative method, objective observation. There changed a focus from legal-formal institutions to people's behaviour and their effects on political processes as well as political systems. Roy Macridis's name in this aspect very popular especially in his book "The Study of Comparative Government" (1955), he criticised the traditional approach for not emphasizing on non-formal political processes. Some of the other prominent political scientist in the 20th century that concentrate traditional studies into a systematic study are Ogg, Zink, Munro, C.F. Strong, Herman Finer, Almond, Powell, Blondel, A.R. Ball, Coleman, David Apter, S E Finer and others. In 1954, Gabriel Almond and his fellow worker from American Social Science Research Council's Committee on Comparative Politics decided to develop a theory and methodology that includes and compares political systems of all kinds such as primitive or advanced, democratic or non-democratic, western or non-western.

As said earlier, the emergence of new states broadens the comparison among states. Gradually the notion of State got replaced by the concept of 'System' and scholars began to focus on social and cultural institutions of non-western countries. Rather than a study of legal powers of the institutions, the new study enquires how they perform their functions, their role in the execution of policies along with making a comparison with different formal & informal institutions. Here raises the idea of structural-functionalism where certain functions are common to all societies but the comparative study was started how different structures perform these functions[10].

In the 1960s, as Wiarda said the new nations became living laboratories for the study of social and political change. During this time, there is a development of new approaches in the field of comparative politics such as political culture, political socialisation, developmentalism, dependency and under dependency, beaurocratic-authoritarianism and later transition to democracy etc. Moreover, this period shows the expanding of some universalistic models that claim applicability irrespective of cultural nature, scope and ideological differences. These are like David Easton's political system, Karl Deutch's social mobilisation, Edward Shil's 'Centre and Periphery'; theories of modernisation by David Apter, Rokkan, Eisenstand; theories of development by Gabriel Almond, Lucian Pye, Sidney Verba etc. Another significant writing in 1960 was 'Politics of Developing Areas' by Almond and Coleman that herald the emergence of new 'Comparative Politics Movement'. 'Developmentalism' in this period became a dominant paradigm that derived from the USA's interest in studying 'developing countries' to counter Marxism-Leninism for striving non-communist way to development[11]

But in 1970 onwards developmentalism faced criticism for supporting universalistic frameworks. The main challenges to developmentalism were –dependency and corporatism. The critiques stressed on the answers to the underdevelopment of the developing countries. Dependency theories mainly criticised developmentalism for overlooking domestic class factors; international market and power factors in development. It emphasised that the development of the already developed nations are gained at the cost of non-western nations.

They asserted that non-western countries were undeveloped but it was the diffusion of the capitalist system of the industrialised countries that make them underdeveloped. This criticism was reflected in Andre Gundre Frank's book "Capitalism and Underdevelopment in Latin America" (1967), Walter Rodney's "How Europe Underdeveloped Africa" (1972) and Malcolm Caldwell's "The Wealth of Some Nations" (1979).

Marxist critics of the dependency theory talked about that the nature of exploitation through surplus extraction is not only confined to the national arena but as an aspect of the difficult pattern of alliances between the bourgeoisie of the core and the indigenous bourgeoisie of the periphery that sustained in a worldwide capitalist system. The corporatist approach criticised developmentalism for favouring eurocentric viewpoint of development that followed a formal, structured and universalistic model of development. It is criticised from applying one theory to all settings irrespective of third world countries.

In the late 1970s marked the decline of developmental theory and a number of theories emerged into the discipline of comparative politics such as bureaucratic-authoritarianism, transition to democracy, structural adjustments, neoliberalism and privatisation. Almond who argued in the 1950s that the state should be replaced by the political system that also continued till in the writings of David Easton as the main theme of political study. But gradually state regained its attention in the work of Ralph Miliband's "The State in Capitalist Society (1969, Nicos Poulantaz's" State, Power, Socialism (1978), in the writings of Peter Evans, Theda Skocpol.

Most of the developments of comparative political analysis took place between1960s to 1980s. In the late 20th century, reasserted interest in historical inquiry in the social sciences in the works of Theda Skocpol and M.Somer's 'The Use of Comparative History in Macro social Inquiry', Comparative Studies in Society and History, 1980; P. Abrams, Historical Sociology, 1982 etc. Moreover, newly importance was given on specific political cultures, institutions and focus on grand systems got weakened that led to the start of comparisons of smaller systems or regions.

After the disintegration of the Soviet Union, there arose recognition of the victory of liberal democracy as the final of government. It was reflected in the article 'End of history' (1989) and the book 'The End of History and the Last Man'(1992). At the same time, there was another significant development in the late 20th century was globalisation. With the advent of globalisation led to the triumph of capitalism. Consequently, the study of civil society gained significance that emphasised on the protection of individual rights in the modern capitalist world.

In this way, with time, the knowledge and understanding achieved to help the growth of Comparative Politics as an indispensably essential and popular subject of study. Earlier from a legal-institutional study, it transformed into a behavioural, functional and scientific study of all political systems and this prominently revolutionized the range of the study that even. continues today. However, it contributed comparative politics to be regarded as an autonomous subject within the comprehensive domain of Political Science.

Major Approaches of Comparative Politics

Traditional Approaches

The traditional approaches to Political Science were broadly predominant until the occurrence of the Second World War. These approaches were mainly associated with the traditional outlook of politics which underlined the study of the state and government. Consequently, traditional approaches are principally concerned with the study of the organization and activities of the state and principles and the ideas which motivate political organizations and activities. These approaches were normative and ethical. According to the philosophers of the traditional approach, the study of Political Science should be limited to the formal structures of the government, laws, rules and regulations.

Philosophical Approach

The ancient approach to the study of politics is philosophical. A philosophical approach is a conventional approach to study politics. Typically, the study of politics was dominated by philosophical considerations on universal political values that were viewed as essential to the just state and the good state. Several Greek philosophers such as Plato and Aristotle were the originators of this approach. This approach conditions that values are inseparable from facts. It is primarily an ethical and normative study of politics, hence is concerned with what 'should be' or 'ought to be'. This approach seeks to understand our fundamental nature and aim as human beings, recognizing principles and criteria of right conduct in political life. It followed the logical method where an investigator has his values and determined philosophies. The normative-philosophical approach is the oldest and the least scientific approach to the study of politics.

Historical Approach

This approach states that political theory can be only understood when the historical factors are taken into consideration. It highlights on the study of the history of every political phenomenon to analyse any situation. Political theorists like Machiavelli, Sabine and Dunning believed that politics and history are strongly inter-related, and therefore, the study of politics always should have a historical viewpoint. Sabine considered that Political Science should include all those subjects which have been discussed in the writings of different political thinkers since Plato. History defines about the past as well as links it with the present events. Without studying the past political events, institutions and political environment, the analysis of the present would remain largely imperfect. History communicates researchers how government, political parties and many other institutions worked, their successes and failures and from these, they receive lessons which guide them in determining the future course of action

Institutional Approach

Institutional approaches are an ancient and important approach to the study of Political Science. These approaches mainly deal with the formal aspects of government and politics. Institutional approach is concerned with the study of the formal political structures like the legislature, executive, and judiciary. It focused on the rules of the political system, the powers of the various institutions, the legislative bodies, and how the constitution worked. The study of institutions has been dominant not only to the arena of comparative politics but to the political science field as a whole. Many writers have argued that institutions have shaped political behaviour and social change. These authors have taken an "institutionalist" approach which treats institutions as independent variables. In the last twenty-five years, the field of comparative politics has experienced the advent of the "new institutionalism," which developed in reaction to the behavioural perspectives that exercise a significant influence on the field during the 1960s and 1970s.

The new institutionalism body can be divided into three analytical approaches: Historical institutionalism, rational choice institutionalism Sociological institutionalism. These three theoretical approaches developed autonomously from each other.

The institutional approach to political analysis emphasises on the formal structures and agencies of government. It originally concentrated on the development and operation of legislatures, executives and judiciaries. As the approach developed, however, the list is extended to include political parties, constitutions, bureaucracies, interest groups and other institutions which are more or less enduringly engaged in politics[12].

Legal Approach

Traditional approaches also include legal or juridical approach. This approach considers the state as the principal institution for the creation and enforcement of laws. Therefore, this approach is associated with the legal process, legal bodies or institutions, and the judiciary. In this approach, the study of politics is mixed with legal processes and institutions. The supporters of this approach are Cicero, Bodin, Hobbes, John Austin, Dicey and Henry Maine.

Criticism of traditional approaches

The traditional approaches have unsuccessful to recognise the role of the individuals who are important in shaping the nature of politics. Individuals are important performers of both national and international politics. The effort is engaged to the institutions. It is criticised that emphasised solely on institutions and overlooking individuals cannot be considered as proper methods to study politics. Moreover, the traditionalists are limited within the institutions. Political researchers in the modern world are not interested to bind their study of politics within institutions. They have exposed the role of the environment into which is included international politics, multinational corporations, non-governmental organisations or trans-national bodies etc. In this way, the traditional approach is prejudiced and incomplete. It has not the capability to see the essentials which are prominent in the contemporary age. It is supposed that traditional analysis is unsuitable for all types of political systems both Western and non-Western. Thus, to overcome this lacking, the political scientists of the post-Second World War era have established a modern approach which is quite comprehensive.

Modern Approach

The political philosophers, later on, understood the necessity to study politics from a different perspective. Thus, to overcome the paucities of the traditional approaches, various new approaches have been promoted by the new political intellectuals. These new approaches are considered as the "modern approaches" to the study of Political Science. These approaches are mainly concerned with the scientific study of politics. Major characteristics of Modern Approaches are they conclude from empirical data, not concentrating only on the study of political structures and its historical analysis, inter-disciplinary nature.

Sociological Approaches

The sociological approach to politics is very popular. It includes human behaviour including political behaviour, group behaviour and attitude of group, culture, society. Most eminent philosophers are MacIver, David Easton, Almond. Many thinkers apprehended that the state is more of a social than a political institution. It means the social challenge is important to understand the political behaviours of an individual[13]. Another important area that belongs to this approach is culture. "Culture refers to the totality of what is learned by individuals as members of society, it is a way of life a mode of thinking, acting and feeling." Culture in several ways impacts on the political behaviour of individuals which is the domain of investigation of political scientists. However, Researchers of politics are attentive of political culture which is composed of the attitudes, beliefs, emotions and values of a society that relate to the political system and its political issues. So far as culture is concerned, it is the subject matter of both sociology and political science.

Psychological Approach

There is a strong connection between politics and psychology. Psychologists usually study the political behaviour of individuals and factors leading to such behaviour. They also concern why certain individuals behave in a certain way. Moreover, psychology studies the behaviour, attitude of the voter and after studying various aspects, the researchers draw conclusions which very often assist the purpose of political leaders. There are motives, likes and dislikes behind every type of political activity. So politics cannot be isolated from psychology. Even in international politics, the effect of psychology is evident. The big powers are involved in power politics to establish their power and boost their image in international society. This is completely a psychological concern.

Quantitative Approach

This approach is called a statistical approach. It is defined as the practice of numerical data to the process of describing and analysing the political phenomenon. Descriptive or prescriptive analysis is not sufficient. The supporters of this approach reveal that researchers have to prove scientifically the validity of a proposition by making use of graph, table, and charts. Several writers practice this approach in comparative politics such as Gallup, Charles Merriam, Harold Gosnell, and Lubell etc.

System Approach

The notion of Systems Theory dates back to 1920s. Ludwig Von Bertallanfy is considered as the earliest advocate of the general systems theory. In the 1960s, the systems theory became an important tool to assess and inspect key factors in Political Science. Among political scientists, David Easton has been the first to apply this theory to political analysis and opine that a political system operates within the social environment. Society influences in an economic, religious way that do shape the political process.

The political system operates within an environment. The environment produces demands from different parts of society. Different demands have different levels of support. Easton assumed that both 'demands' and 'supports' create 'inputs.' The political system receives these inputs from the environment and after considering several factors, the government accept the appropriate demands among them and reject others. The inputs are converted into 'outputs' by the decision-makers in the form of policies, decisions, rules, regulations and laws. The 'outputs' flow back into the environment through a 'feedback' mechanism, giving rise to fresh 'demands.' Accordingly, it is a cyclical process. David Easton, G. A. Almond and Morton A. Kaplan are credited for applying this approach in Political Science. According to this theory, political behaviour is conceived as a system and the political system is well-defined as "Authoritative allocation of values with a threat or actual use of deprivations to make them binding on all". It is the system of interactions to be found in independent societies which performs the functions of integration and adaptation. A political system executes these to maintain itself.

Simultaneous Approach

Simulation means the study with the support of image construction or model building. Such evidence is used in political communication, decision making and game theory. The political communication approach formulated by Karl Deutsch lays stress on how one part of the system influences another by sending messages or transmitting the information. According to this approach, politics and government act as processes of coordinating human efforts towards the attainment of some goals (J. C. Johari, 1982).

Decision-Making Approach is another example of a simulation approach. Decision-making approach searches the qualities of decision-makers as well as the type of influence the individuals have on the decision-makers. Richard Synder and Charles Lindblom are proponents of this approach.

Behavioural Approach

Behaviouralism emerged during the middle of the 20th century. Behviouralism emphasises on the scientific, objective and value-free study of the political incidences as conditioned by the environment, mainly the behaviour of the individuals involved in that phenomena. Behaviouralism is the development of method against traditional political science which did not consider human behaviour as an important factor in politics.

David Easton has identified certain key features of behaviouralism which are regarded as its intellectual foundations. These are:

Regularities: This approach believes that there are certain regularities in political behaviour which can be stated in generalizations or theories to interpret and predict political phenomena. In a certain situation, the Political behaviour of individuals may be more or less common that may help to examine a political situation as well as to predict the future political phenomena.

Verification: The behaviouralists want to accept phenomena by stressing on testing and verifying. They are of the view that if the phenomenon is not tested then it will not be scientific.

Techniques: The behaviouralists stress on the practice of those research methods which create valid, reliable and comparative data. A researcher must make use of developed tools like sample surveys, mathematical models etc.

Quantification: After collecting data, the researcher should measure and quantify those data.

Values: The behaviouralists focused on the separation of facts from values. They consider that to do unbiased research, one has to be value-free. It means that the researcher should not have any preconceived idea or a biased view.

Systematization: According to the behaviouralists, research in Political Science must be systematic. Theory and research should go together.

Pure Science: Another feature of behaviouralism is to make Political Science pure science. It believes that the study of Political Science should be confirmed by evidence.

Integration: Behaviouralists stated that political Science should not be separated from various other social sciences such as history, sociology and economics. This approach indicates that political happenings are moulded by various other factors in the society and hence, it would be inappropriate to separate Political Science from other disciplines.

Post behaviourism: After some time, it started to understand that unlike natural sciences, generalizations could not be made in the field of social sciences. Therefore, a new thought emerged that criticise behaviouralists for ignoring values. David Easton this aspect very prominent. In1969, David Easton stated that because of excessive use of mathematics, Political Science viewed more of mathematics instead of social science and that it does not enquire the contemporary world.

Marxist Approach

Marxian approach to politics is not limited to the writings of Marx, Engels and Lenin but all those of a congregation of later writers such as Luxemburg, Trotsky, Gramsci and many others. Further, an explicitly 'political' treatise cannot be found in the whole range of classical Marxist texts. Miliband indicated that "a Marxist politics had to be constructed or reconstructed from the mass of variegated and fragmented material which forms the corpus of Marxism."

Marx views on Individual and Society

Marx stated that Individual has no identity without society. He called that "society does not consist of individuals, but expresses the sum of interrelations, the relations within which these individuals stand." In the case of society, Marxists stressed that all societies in history have been class societies. All class societies are categorised by supremacy and conflict which are based on specific, concrete features of their mode of production. Class domination has been a historical process suggesting a constant attempt on the part of the dominant classes to maintain and extend their power on society.

Marx on Politics

Marxist considered that politics can be understood only concerning the nature of prevailing societal conflict and domination. The political life processes are considered as part of 'superstructure' based on the economic structure of society. According to Marx, Politics, economics, culture and ideology are all inseparably linked. The 'forces of production' at a particular stage of historical development, are consistent by definite 'relations of production' that illustrate the society. Both constitute the economic foundation of society.

Structural-Functional Approach

These approaches highlight structures and functions. Gabriel Almond was an advocate of this approach. He described political systems as a special arrangement of interaction that exists in all societies performing certain functions. According to him, the main attributes of a political system are comprehensiveness, inter-dependence and existence of boundaries. Like Easton, Almond also believes that all political systems perform input and output functions. The Input functions of political systems are political socialization and recruitment, interest-articulation, interest-aggression and political communication. Almond makes three-fold classifications of governmental output functions relating to policymaking and implementation. These output functions are rulemaking, rule application and rule adjudication.

Communication Theory Approach

This approach scrutinizes how one part of a system affects another by sending messages or information. Robert Weiner first well-defined this approach. Later on, Karl Deutsch developed it and applied it in Political Science. This approach treats the government as the decision-making system that is responsible for overseeing different communication channels. According to Deutsch, the four factors of analysis in communication theory are lead, lag, gain and load.

In this way, Comparative Politics as a sub-discipline of Political Science deals with the prospect of understanding the politics and political process in a comparative outlook. It has a rich legacy that can be drawn back to the earliest political philosophers and has grown gradually with its share of challenges.

Points to Remember

- Comparative Politics has a long-lasting history dating back to the very origin of systematic political studies in ancient Greece and Rome.
- Comparative Politics is necessary for a proper understanding of both international relations and foreign policy.
- The scope of Comparative Politics includes the study of all the formal and informal, governmental and extra-governmental, which are directly or indirectly involved in the struggle for power taking place in each state.
- The study of Comparative politics dates back by the studies done by the Greek philosopher Aristotle. Aristotle studied the constitutions of 150 states and classified them into a typology of governments.
- Comparative Politics holds analytical and Imperial research that is considered a value-free empirical study that rejects normative (value-laden), descriptive methods of comparative government.

Further Readings

A. Roy, 'Comparative Method and Strategies of Comparison', *Punjab Journal of Politics*, 2001 Vol. xxv (2), pp. 1-15.

J. Blondel, 'Then and Now: Comparative Politics', *Political Studies*, 1996, Vol. 47 (1), pp. 152-160.

J. Kopstein, and M. Lichbach, (eds), *Comparative Politics: Interests, Identities, and Institutions in a Changing Global Order*, (Cambridge: Cambridge University Press, 2005), pp. 1-5; 16-36; 253-290.

M. Mohanty,'*Comparative Political Theory and Third World Sensitivity*', *Teaching Politics,* 1975, pp. 22-38.

N. Chandhoke, 'Limits of Comparative Political Analysis', *Economic and Political Weekly*, 1996, Vol. 31 (4), January 27, pp. 2-8.

Multiple Chioce Questions

(a) In his work "The Politics", who comparaed different constitutions, by introducing a famous typology based on two criteria: the number of rulers (one, few, many) and the nature of the political regime (good or corrupt).

(i) Plato (ii) Aristotle

(iii) Socrate (iv) Kant

(b) Traditional Appraoches are concerned with –

(i) normative and ethical (ii) Value laden

(iii) Subjective (iv) All

(c) Who has identified the key features of behaviouralism- Regularities, Verification, Techniques, Quantification as its intellectual foundations?

(i) David Easton (ii) Herman Finner

(iii) Devid Apter (iv) R.G Neumann.

(d) Who defined Comparative Politics as "Comparative Politics is concerned with significant regularities, similarities and differences in the working of political institutions and political behaviour."?

(i) Aristotle (ii) M. Curtis

(iii) David Easton (iv) Peter Mair and Richard Rose

(e) Who wrote the book 'Modern Democracies'(1921)?

(i) Carl J. Friedrich (ii) M. Duverger

(iii) Roberto Michaels (v) James Bryce.

(f) In which year Andre Gundre Frank wrote the book "Capitalism and Underdevelopment in Latin America".

(i) 1966 (ii) 1967.

(iii) 1968 (iv) 1970

(g) Who formulated the Political Communication Approach ?

(i) Karl Deutsch (ii) Karl Marx.

(iii) Lipset (iv) All

(h) Ralph Miliband's wrote the book-

(i) The State in Capitalist Society (1969)

(ii) Theory and Practice of Modern Governments(1932)

(iii) Constitutional Government and Democracy'(1937),

(iv) Comparative Politics(1972)

(i) 'The Intellectual Father of Behavioualism' is

(i) Charles . E. Meerriam (ii) David Easton

(iii) Laswell. (iv) None

Notes

1. "Definitions for Comparative Politics", Retrieved from https://www.definations.net/defination/compartive+politics.
2. *Ibid.*
3. Tanvi Priya, "Comparative Politics: Meaning, Scope and Its Evolution", *Political Science.*Retrieved from http://www.politicalsciencenotes.com/politics/comparative-politics-meaning-scope-and-its-evolution-political-system/1382.
4. *Ibid.*
5. *Ibid.*
6. Civil Service India, "Comparative Politics : Nature and Approaches".
7. Chilcote, Ronald H., "Introduction, in Ronald H.Chilcote", in *Theories of Comparative Politics: The Search for a Paradigm Reconsidered*, 2nd edition. (Boulder: Westview Press, 1994), p. 4.
8. IGNOU, "Unit-1, Nature, Scope of Comparative Study Politics"
9. Peter Muir, "Comparative Politics- An Overview", (London: Oxford University Press), p.315.
10. Howard J.Wiarda, "Is Comparative Politics Dead? Rethinking the Field in the Post-Cold War Era", *Third World Quarterly*, Vol. 19, no. 5), p. 937.
11. J.C Johari, "Comparative Politics", (New Delhi: Sterling Publishers, 1982).

12 J.C Jorhari, "Comparative Politics", New Delhi: Sterling Publication, 1982).

Chapter - 2

Going Beyond Euro-centrism

What is Euro-Centrism

Eurocentrism means focusing on European culture or history to the explosion of a wider view of the world. It was means western-centrism. It was developed to describe the outlook of the world from a strictly European perspective and with European experiences in mind. The termEuro-centrism dates back to the late 1970s and become prevalent during the 1990s, especially in the context of decolonization and development aid and humanitarian aid offered by industrialized countries or the first world to developing countries. However, it is a political term coined that referring to the notion of European exceptionalism, a world view centered on western civilization as it had developed during the height of the European colonial empires since the early modern period. Generally, it perceives as a universal phenomenon that asserts the superiority of European cultural values over those of non-European societies. They are considering European culture as rational, scientific, and progressive. They are usually discrediting Orientalism and consider 'Eastern' culture as irrational, superstitious, traditional, and backward. It attempts to impose a theory of progress and development, i.e, modernization theory and treated that the path to modernization, development & progress is the same for all nations as it was for 'Europe'. It also believes in the western model that is based on 'western values' i.e, individuality, equality, democracy, human rights, free market, secularism, social justice, etc. are the pillars of solving any difficulties having different histories, cultures, and society[1] . Two assertions constituted eurocentrism- first, the history of modernity that consists of the transmission of the western accomplishment and secondly that European development can be understood as insufficient without reference to extra- European events Eurocentrism has been a particularly important concept in development studies. Brohman (1995) argued that Eurocentrism "perpetuated intellectual dependence on a restricted group of prestigious Western academic institutions that determine the subject matter and methods of research"[2]. Over the past years, the idea that we live in a globalized world has considerably gained prominent. Globalization led by the capitalist free-market economy and liberal democracy is the manifestation of Eurocentrism in present times.

Beyond Euro-centrism

Beyond Euro-centrism severely criticized Eurocentrism for the universalization of European norms. One of the critiques like Andre Gunder Frank criticized some Western scholars for their ideas that non-Western areas lack outstanding contributions in history, economy, ideology, politics, and culture compared with the West[3]. These scholars believed that the same contribution made by the West gives Westerners an advantage of endo-genetic momentum which is pushed towards the rest of the world, but Frank believed that the Oriental countries also contributed to the human civilization on their perspectives. Especially after decolonization, the politics of Asia and developing countries generally have constitutional monarchies, absolute monarchies, one-party state, federal states, dependent territories, liberal democracies. Many of the political culture in Asia today is affected by colonialism and imperialism of the past. With some states having close links with their former colonial governors while others involved in bitter independence struggle the consequences of which continue to be felt. Political Scientists argue that Africa had never freed itself from domination by the west[4]. In the 21st century, the relationship between the West and Africa has been primarily of exploitation.

The arrival of western powers had an impact on Southeast Asian political and public administration as well. The institutions for a modern state such as state beaurocracy, courts of law were created.

Then South East Asian countries were transformed from a traditional kingdom into a modern nation-state. In most southeast Asian countries, the colonial- bureaucratic model offers the guiding principles for modernizing state administration which replaced the traditional local administration. According to Wilson, there were two main types of colonial governments in South Asia- liberal colonial governments and repressive colonial governments[5]. The British and the Americans were the two liberal colonial governments at that time. The British colonized Malaysia, Singapore, and Burma; while the Philippine was under the American rule. In Malaysia, the British established the bureaucratic model of administration based on the concept of hierarchical loyalty. After getting independence the Malaysian governments also adopted this model. Similarly, the Singaporean government followed the British style of public administration after its separation from Malaysia in 1965[6].

While Malasia, Singapore, and Burma followed the British parliamentary system of government, the Philippines adopted the American political model[7]. It was formed under the American style political system with including the separation of power, the direct election of the president, and the system of checks of trade and balances. The British and Americans brought their colonies the rule of law, civil liberties, and rights in politics.

People have limited liberty under the control of the repressive government because colonial power always regarded their interests as superior. Although Thailand was the only state in the region that was not under Colonial rule, its administrative system started to alter towards the western beaurocratic, especially under the regime of King Chulalongkorn. He established the Beaurocracy and put that society on the way to political reform with the use of the western model. The reforms based on the uniform standards of public service, separate public office, and personal life. As a result, Thailand transformed from a traditional kingdom to a modern state. In this way, the western beaurocratic model of administration was established in South East Asia. Apart from this, if we see that after globalization, the emerging powers have increasingly been their influence to challenge the legitimacy of the post- Second World Order, manifesting a multipolar conceptions. Countries like Russia, China, India, Brazil or Turkey challenge the western world and building regional groupings that can potentially create a global equilibrium between themselves.

Points to Remember

- It perceives as a universal phenomenon that asserts the superiority of European cultural values over those of non-European societies.
- They are usually disbelieving Orientalism and consider 'Eastern' culture as irrational, superstitious, traditional, and backward.
- Beyond Euro-centrism severely criticized Eurocentrism for the universalization of European norms.
- Frank believed that the Oriental countries also contributed to the human civilization on their perspectives specially after decolonisation.

Further Reading

Brohman, John, "Universalism, Eurocentrism, and Ideological Bias in Development Studies: From Modernisation to Neoliberalism". *Third World Quarterly*, 16(1), 1995: 121–140.

Peter Gran, "*Beyond Euro-centrism: A New View Modern World History*", (New York: Syracuse University Press, 1996).

Multiple Choice Questions

(a) Eurocentrism basically means-

(i) Eastern- centrism (ii) Western-centrism

(iii) Western-Eastern centrism (iv) All

(b) Eurocentrismcriticises the Eastern Culture as -

(i) Irrational (ii) Superstitious

(iii) traditional and backward (iv) All

(c) Liberal Colonial Governments and Repressive Colonial governments- types of colonial governments in South Asia- According to whom?

(i) Wilson (ii) David Easton

(iii) Karl Duetch (iv) None.

(d) Beyond Eurocentrism criticized Euro-centrism for-

(i) Universalization of European norms

(ii) Orientalism

(iii) Euresian – centric

(iv) All.

Notes

1. Arun Kumar Pokhrel, "Eurocentrism",in *Encyclopedia of Global Justice*, ed. Deen K. Chatterjee (Switzerland: Springer, 2011).
2. Brohman, John, "Universalism, Eurocentrism, and Ideological Bias in Development Studies: From Modernisation to Neoliberalism". *Third World Quarterly*, 1995, 16(1), pp. 121–140.
3. Andre Gunder Frank , "*Re Orient: global economy in the Asian Age*", (Berkeley: University of California 1998).
4. Amin S, "Euro-centrism", (New York: Russel M, 1989).
5. Lander E, "Euro-centrism and colonialism in Latin American social thought", *Nepantla Views South*, 1(3): 519-532.
6. Peter Gran, "*Beyond Euro-centrism: A New View Modern World History*", (New York: Syracuse University Press, 1996).
7. Dussel E, "Beyond Eurocentrism: the World-system and the limits of modernity", *The Cultures of Globalisation*, ed. Jameson F, Miyoshi M (Durham: Duke University Press, 1998).

UNIT - II

HISTORICAL CONTEXT OF MODERN GOVERNMENT

Chapter - 3

Capitalism: Meaning and Development: Globalisation

Capitalism is an economic system and an ideology in which the means of production and distribution are privately owned. Here development occurs through the accumulation and reinvestment of profits in a free market.The purest form of capitalism is free market or laissez-faire capitalism where individuals are unrestrained. They may decide where to invest, what to produce or sell, and at which prices to exchange goods and services. No external control or checks in the marketplace.

Private property rights are central to capitalism. In this system, the person who owns the property is entitled to any value associated with that property. Once owned, the only legitimate means of transferring property are through voluntary exchange, inheritance, etc.

In this way, in a capitalist market economy decision making and investment are determined by the owners of the factors of production in financial as well as capital market. In it, prices and the distribution of goods are mainly determined by competition in the market.Under capitalism prices and wages are determined by the forces of supply and demand.

In the words of Prof. R.T. Bye, "Capitalism is that system of economic organization in which free enterprise, competition and private ownership of property generally prevail".

According to G.D.H. Cole, "Capitalism is a system of production for profit under which instruments and materials of production are privately owned, the work is done mainly by hired labor, the product belonging to the capitalist owner or owners."

When wa talk about forms of Colonialism, economists, political economists, and historians have agreed to various perspectives in their study of capitalism and have acknowledged different forms of it in practice.

Laissez-faire or Free Market Capitalism: It is an economic system in which transactions between private parties are free from government intervention such as regulation, privileges tariffs, and subsidies.

Welfare Capitalism: It is a capitalism that includes social, welfare policies. It also involves the practice of business providing welfare services to their employees.

State Capitalism: It is an economic system in which the state carries out commercial economic activity and the means of production are organized and managed state-owned business enterprises.

Capitalism and Its Characteristics

There are several categories of economic systems adopted by nations, one of them is capitalism. It can be very complex to understand an economic system like capitalism. Although there are different levels of commitment to the ideals of capitalism, some are common traits among all the capitalist.Capitalist ownership possesses two meanings- one is the owner controls the factors of production; another is they attained their income from their ownership. This allows them to maximize profit.

Firstly, it is an economic system in which every individual in his capacity as a consumer, producer, and the resource owner is engaged in economic activity with a degree of economic freedom.

Capitalism mostly a two-class system. Historically this type of society is featured by the spilt between two classes of individuals- the

Capitalist class that owns the means for producing and distributing goods representing the owners and the Working Class who sell their labor to the capitalist class in exchange for wages.

In a capitalist system, the economy is carried out by the individuals or corporations who own and operate companies, make decisions regarding the use of resources. Here exist a 'division of labour' that allows for specialization, typically occurring through education and training. It further divided into sub-classes, i.e., the middle class.

Capitalism rest on the application of private property rights, which provide incentives for investment in and suitable use of productive capital. Moreover, capitalism established historically out of previous systems of feudalism and mercantilism in Europe, and intensely extended industrialization and the large-scale availability of mass-market consumer goods.

Capitalism requires a free market economy to succeed. It denotes the distribution of goods and services according to the laws of supply and demand.

The market mechanism is another significant characteristic feature of a capitalist economy. It is also termed as a price mechanism. Under the capitalist economy, the profit that is linked with the market mechanism guides the allocation of resources. Under this, the whole economic system rests on the market mechanism.

Market participants freely decide how to allocate capital and what prices to set for goods. In it, Capitalist societies consider markets should be left alone to work with no government intervention.

Pure capitalism can be distinguished with pure socialism where means of production are controlled by state-owned and in mixed economies there lies the combination of pure capitalism and pure socialism.

In practices of capitalism, typically includes some sort of "Crony capitalism" because of the demands from business for favorable government involvement and government incentive to intervene in the economy.

Origins of Capitalism

The history of capitalism can be traced back to early forms of merchant capitalism practiced in Western Europe during the Middle Ages (between 5th to 15th centuries). It began to develop into its modern form during the early modern period in the countries of North-Western Europe, especially the Netherland and England.

Crisis of the 14th Century

According to some historians the modern capitalist system has its origin in the crisis of the 14th century. It was a conflict between the land-owning aristocracy and the agricultural producers or serfs. Serfs had to produce for lords and therefore, had no interest in technological innovation. Because lords were not producing to sell on the market, there was no competitive pressure for them to innovate. Finally, lords expanded their power and wealth through military means.

The democratic crisis of the 14th century upset this arrangement. This crisis had several causes-agricultural productivities reached its technological limitations and bad weather led to the Great Famine of 1315-1317. The crisis had consequences for the church, state, European society, and the black death of 1346-1353 led to a population crash. These factors led to declining agricultural production. In response, feudal lords sought to expand agricultural production by expanding their domains through welfare. Feudalism began to lay some foundation necessary for the development of mercantilism, the precursor of capitalism. Feudalism was mostly confined to Europe and lasted through the 16th century. In this way, the relatively sudden emergence of new technologies and discovering, particularly in agriculture facilitated the growth of capitalism. The most important development at the end of feudalism was the emergence of what Robert Degan calls the dichotomy between wage, earners, and capitalist merchants.

However, only fully emerged in the early modern period between the 16th and 18thcentury the establishment of merchant capitalism under the mercantilism, European merchants backed by state controls succeeded. The mercantilism emphasized state power and viewed that if a state could not supply its materials, it should acquire colonies from which they could be extracted which means that colonies constituted not only sources of supply for raw materials but also markets for finished products.

In the late 18th century, Marx marked the development of the factory system of manufacturing characterized by a complex division of labour between and within work progress and finally establish the global domination of the capitalist mode of production.

By the mid 19th century, Britain was firmly committed to the notion of free trade and the first era of globalization began. In this era, Britain embraced liberalism, competition, and the development of a market economy. Globalization in this period was decisively checked by 19th-century imperialism. Several major challenges to capitalism appeared in the earlier part of the 20th century. The Russian revolution in 1917 established the first socialist state in the world; a decade later the great depression triggered increasing criticism of the existing capitalist system. The economic recovery of the world's leading capitalist economics in the period following the end of the Great Depression and World War II led to the discussion of capitalism's external decline. The state began to play an increasingly prominent role to regulate the capitalist system throughout much of the world. Moreover, in 1991 the collapse of the Soviet Union brought further evidence superiority of market capitalism over a planned economy. However, since the last part of the 20th century, the internationalization of finance has posed the question of state sovereignty because of the growing globalization of capital. In this way, capitalism has grown over the years. In this century, often the capitalist system got replaced by free enterprise and private enterprise. At the same time, many aspects of capitalism have come under attack from the anti-globalization movement that mainly opposed to corporate capitalism. Another strong criticism comes from environmentalist have argued that capitalism needs continual economic growth that exhausts the finite natural resources of Earth. Some others also argue that neoliberalism, the ideological backbone of contemporary globalized capitalism through enhanced global trade but also led to the destruction of the traditional way of life.

Globalization

Globalization is a process, a strategy concerning an irresistible movement for the good of all the people of the world. The term 'globalization' popularised by Theodore Levitt in 1983. It is a comprehensive term that involves economic, socio-cultural, and political aspects. In the words of Giddens, "It is the intensification of worldwide relations with link distant localities in a way that local happenings are shaped by events occurring many miles away and vice-versa.'

According to M. Water, 'Globalisation is a social process to which the constraints of geography and social and cultural arrangements diminish in which people become increasingly aware that they receding.'

Thus globalization is a system in which human beings are no longer like a part of the isolated communities that are themselves linked through narrow channels of diplomatic relations and trade.

Salient features of globalization

The pace of economic transformation has created a new world of politics. The world economy is more interdependent than ever and trade& finances growing significantly. Nowadays, states cannot control their economies.

Communications have primarily revolutionized the way we deal with the rest of the world. Electronic communications led to social progress tremendously. Moreover, the world is becoming more homogenous because differences between people are lessening nowadays. The world shares common cultures that advance integrity among the people.

Time and space appear to be collapsing. Our old ideas of geographical space are undermined by the speed of modern communications and media. People are beginning to think globally and act locally.

Though globalization has not dissolved the state but someway has not left it untouched either. Nowadays the role of the state in the super-territorial sphere should be examined.

Thus, globalization offers social and economic relations concerning distanceless and borderless qualities that human lives are increasingly played out in the world as a single space.

Dimensions of Globalisation

There are several dimensions of globalization – economic; socio-cultural and political. As economic affairs, globalization refers to a process of deepening economic integration, increasing economic openness, and growing economic interconnectedness between countries in the world economy. As economic self-sufficiency can not be possible by any country so states have to be economically integrated. Economic globalization has both positive and negative effects. On the positive side, it facilitates the reduction of tariffs, in the pattern of investment, new rules of safeguards. Moreover, the integration of financial markets has an impact on the international monetary system. On the negative side, such development only benefits the rich section of people and advanced countries that harm mostly the resourceful poor underdeveloped nations. In this way, the poor countries cannot compete with the industrialized nations and they are used by the developed countries for their surplus products.

Socio-cultural dimension referrers to a process whereby information, communications that have been created in part of the world and reach into a world-wide flow which leads to cultural divergence between regions as well as individuals. With the emergence of transnational companies, cultural globalization is also driven by information revolution such as satellite communication, information technology, etc. But its challenge can be seen in the case of religious fundamentalists and the growth of multiculturalism. It led to the emergence of the concept of identity politics, politics of recognition, and has been a remote connection with the growing threat of cross-border terrorism that cost thousands of human life. So while globalization denotes cultural homogenization, at the same time multiculturalism stresses the concept of indigenization that struggles for preserving their distinct culture.

Political dimension and impact on state sovereignty is another aspect of globalization. The political aspect of globalization emphasis on the role of global structures and processes of rulemaking and problem solving, the maintenance of security and order in the world system through global platforms.Apart from this, globalization is evident due to the development of many international organizations such as the United Nations, International Labour Organisation, International Monetary Fund, WTO, and regional organizations like the European Union, ASEAN (Association of South East Asian Nations). These organizations exercise their jurisdiction over a defined area along with the member states and sometimes intervene. So the state and its 'absolute' sovereignty are facing major challenges that changed the nature of politics and governance. It mostly shifted from 'state-centric geopolitics' to 'Geocentric global politics'. Moreover, global powers diminish the ability of governments to monopoly control their economics and societies. In this way, though states are the principal actors in the international arena, globalization facilitates new ways to self- governing and new responsibilities.The world communities to assert adequacy of global institutional arrangements and to suggest how they should be reformed and readjustment. Globalization transforming sovereignty into 'shared sovereignty' that promotes greater integration as opposed to the traditional concept of sovereignty,

Transformationalists in this respect believe that nation-states are transforming in response to the requirements of globalization and its complexities. However. They opine that a system of global governance is needed to deal with global problems. In this regard, it is considered that the state's role in making decisions, and their ability to control the population has also increased. Although there is growing global governance and regulations, the sovereign state is still not undermined even its role is changing. The new standardized rules accompanied by agreements between countries can only be realized if there are territorial agencies that can implement them locally and have the power to do so.

Thus, globalization has changed world phenomena and in a globalized world, the transformed sovereignty of states gives them the power and authority to act in the best interests of their people. But taking into account all the factors and influences, sovereignty still plays an essential role in this regard.

Points to Remember

- Capitalism established historically out of previous systems of feudalism and mercantilism in Europe, and intensely extended industrialization and the large-scale availability of mass-market consumer goods.
- The market mechanism is another significant characteristic feature of a capitalist economy.
- Capitalist societies consider markets should be left alone to work with no government intervention.
- The history of capitalism can be traced back to early forms of merchant capitalism practiced in Western Europe during the Middle Ages (between 5th to 15th centuries).
- It began to develop into its modern form during the early modern period in the countries of North-Western Europe, especially the Netherland and England.

Multiple Choice Questions

(a) Forms of Capitalism are-

(i) Laissez-faire or Free Market Capitalism

(ii) Welfare Capitalism

(iii) State Capitalism

(iv) All.

(b) Capitalism basically requires a-

(i) State-controlled economy

(ii) Free- market economy

(iii) Mixed economy

(iv) None.

(c) One of the strong evidence of superiority of market capitalism over a planned economy is-

(i) The collapse of the Soviet Union in 1991

(ii) World War I

(iii) World War II

(iv) Post-behaviouralism

(d) The main reason behind MNCs investments are

(i) To benefit foreign countries

(ii) To provide financial support to the country's government

(iii) For the welfare of underprivileged people

(iv) To increase the assets and earn profits.

(e) When did the government remove the barriers for investment and investment in India?

(i) 1990 (ii) 1991

(iii) 1992 (iv) 1993

(e) Advocates of Economic Globalisation argue-

(i) It involes greater economic flows among different countries of the world

(ii) Greater trade in commodities across the globe.

(iii) It has has led to the flow of ideas across national boundaries.

(iv) All

(f) The bourgeoisie refers to

(i) the monarchy

(ii) the central planners of the Soviet Union

(iii) the capitalist and middle class

(iv) the aristocrats of wealthy nations

(g) Who said, "Globalisation is a social process to which the constraints of geography and social and cultural arrangements diminish in which people become increasingly aware that they receding."

(i) Giddens (ii) M.Water

(iii) F.W. Riggs (iv) David Easton

(h) What is the Full Form of ASEAN –

(i) Association of South East Asian Countries

(ii) Association of South Eastern Asian Nations

(iii) Association of South East Asian Nations

(iv) Association for South East Asian Nations

Further Readings

Hoogvelt, 'History of Capitalism Expansion', in *Globalization and Third World Politics* (London: Palgrave, 2002), pp. 14-28.

E. Wood, 'The Agrarian origin of Capitalism', in *Origin of Capitalism: A Long View*, (London: Verso, 2002), pp. 91-95; 166-181.

G. Ritzer, 'Globalization and Related Process I: Imperialism, Colonialism, Development, Westernization, Easternization', in *Globalization: A Basic Text*, (London: Wiley- Blackwell, 2002), pp. 63-84.

M. Dobb,'Capitalism', in *Studies in the Development of Capitalism*, (London: Routledge and Kegan Paul Ltd, 1950), pp. 1-32.

R. Suresh, '*Economy & Society -Evolution of Capitalism*', (New Delhi :Sage Publications, 2010), pp. 151- 188; 235-268.

Chapter - 4

Socialism: Meaning, Growth, and Development

Socialism is an economic system where everyone in the society equally owns the factors of production.þ That ownership is acquired through a democratically elected government or through a cooperative or a public corporation in which everyone owns shares. As there are four factors of production such as labor, capital goods, natural resources, and in the modern era- entrepreneurship, socialist believed that these factors are valued only for their usefulness to people. They take into account both individual needs and greater social needs. Some of the examples of greater social needs include transportation, defense, education, health care, and preservation of natural resources, etc.[1] Thus, the basic idea of socialism is that "From each according to his ability, to each according to his contribution."

Thus, Socialism is a system that shares economic output equally among all people. It beliefs the collective well-being of the community, rather than individuals particularly. The government distributes resources, giving it greater control over its citizens. Under socialism, workers are no longer exploited because they own the means of production. Profits are distributed equitably among all workers according to their contributions. But the cooperative system also provides for those who can't work. It meets their basic needs for the good of the whole society. The system eliminates poverty. It provides equal access to health care and education. No one is discriminated against. Thus, socialism denotes the means of production that are owned and operated by society/state. Here, profit is used for social welfare and distributed on the principle of equity. However, in practice socialism indicates the means of production that are mostly owned and operated by the state on behalf of society. Private property and enterprise regulated heavily, progressive taxation, welfare state-free or subsidized education, health care, social security, public facilities, income distributed to lessen inequalities.

Growth and Rise of Socialism in Europe

The history of socialism has its roots in the 1789 French Revolution and the changes made by it thereafter. Karl Marx and Friedrich Engels's book 'The Communist Manifesto' (1848) was written only before the Revolutions of 1848 swept Europe, manifesting scientific socialism. Later, in the last third of the 19th century, a socialist democratic party emerged in Europe, represented mainly from Marxism. Eventually, the rise of Socialism was an important event in the 20th century. In the first half of the 20th century, the Soviet Union and the Communist parties of the third international arose around the world mainly to characterize socialism in terms of the Soviet model of economic development and the creation of centrally planned economies directed by a state that owns all the means of production.

Rise of socialism in Eastern and Central Europe started after the Bolshevik revolution in 1917 to 1922, Russia became the first communist state overthrowing the 'Tsar' regime and communist rule started in Russia. The inter-war period between World War I and World War II- 1920-39, the rise of communist parties in East and Central Europe, even strong communist movement arose in France and Italy.In December 1922, USSR was formally formed. Union treaty was signed between Russia, Ukraine, Belarus, and the Transcaucasia (Georgia, Armenia, and Azerbaijan). Apart from this, during 1924-36 there was the inclusion of the Central Asian Republic- Uzbekistan, Tajikistan, Kyrgyzstan, Turkmenistan, and Kazakhstan in the USSR. Later in 1940, Baltic nations such as Lithuania, Latvia, and Estonia and Moldova (emerged from Romania) incorporated into the USSR. Thus it has become a federation of 15 different nations.

During World War II, Germany occupied most of the Eastern European nations, reached almost up to Moscow. But the 'Red Army' of Russia pushed the German army back and won most of Eastern Europe. After World War II, Russia allowed quasi-independent status to Eastern Europe nations as satellite and paramount power was on USSR and accordingly imposed communist regime in central as well as Eastern Europe. Even, Western Europe and the USA accepted Russia's zone of influence and the policy of non-interference. In 1947, Cominform (Communist Information Bureau) was formed by Stalin which was a forum of all the communist parties of Eastern Europe and was to coordinate actions of the communist parties under Soviet direction. In 1955, Warsaw Pact was signed as a collective security defense treaty between the Soviet Union and seven other Eastern Bloc socialist republics of Central and Eastern Europe. British Prime Minister Churchill in a speech mentioned about 'Iron Curtain' that denotes the political, military, and ideological barrier erected by the Soviet Union after World War II to block itself and its satellite states from open contact with the West and non-soviet controlled areas[2]. Later Brezhnev Doctrine was put forth by Soviet leader Leonid Brezhnev that proclaimed any threat to socialist rule in any state of the Soviet bloc in Central and Eastern Europe was a threat to them all, and therefore justified the intervention of fellow socialist states.

Now, we can discuss how some prominent countries of Eastern Europe come into the ambit of the Communist regime and how they become satellite nations. In Poland, after World War II Yalta Conference was held between victor powers- USA, USSR, and United Kingdom to discuss how to re-organize Eastern Europe and how to cut the German territory and redistribute different small nations. By doing this, Poland's territory got harm the most and imposed it with Eastern Germany's part. However, in 1947 after a series of political operations, the communist government was established. Likewise, in Hungary, 1948 communist leader Rakosi overthrew the non-communist elected Government of Zoltan Tildy by manipulation and using force. East Germany was separated by West Germany in 1949 and the Eastern part of Germany was set up a communist-controlled state called the German Democratic Republic (GDR) and West Germany was dominated by capitalist or liberal democratic government is known as Federal Democratic Republic (FDR). In 1945 in Czechoslovakia a coalition Government with Communist party set up and in 1948, communist leader Gottwald took over the government and overthrew all non-communist power. Moreover, in 1945, a Communist-led coalition was elected in Bulgaria and Romania but in 1946 and 1947, communists gained total control and the monarchy was abolished in both the countries respectively.

Fall of Communism

The fall of Communism started in the late 1980s. In 1985, Mikhail Gorbachev took the leadership of the USSR. He was a man of reformist thinking and initiated two significant reforms like 'Glasnost' (means 'Openness' such as open press, can hear and watch foreign country radio, television; criticize government policies openly, multi-party democracy, etc.) and 'Perestroika' (means- 'Restructuring' especially in economic areas- allowing private property to some extent, the government no longer fixed the prices of commodities completely, allowing of private sector industry in a limited manner). But accidently that occurred tremendous change within the next four years. In 1989, a revolution in Eastern Europe began and eventual demise of communist state one by one. By 1988, the Soviets decided to extricate itself as Russian leader Gorbachev asserted the Afghan intervention to support the pro-communist government was an increasing wastage of Russian economy and they were tired of after eight years of intervention. So, Soviet troops began their withdrawal.Then in Poland, infect, at the beginning of the 1980s, the Solidarity party was formed by the workers, intellectuals, students, and peasants that organize mass movements that continued till ten years. In 1989, the victory of this party in free democratic election and Poland was able to form the non-communist government at that time. In Hungary, during the 1956 student-led mass revolution and overthrow the communist regime, but USSR did military action that increases the tension of the cold war and forcefully establishes a communist rule. But in 1989, there is some change in the domestic level where Leninism was abandoned and adopted democratic socialism and multi-party election in 1990. In 1989, in East Germany, massive mass movements were going on and people cross the wall and thus led to the fall of the Berlin War.

This made the unification of East and West Germany and subsequent abandonment of communism. In Czechoslovakia in 1968, 'Prague Spring' reforms were started as a mass protest for the decentralization when the Soviet Union and other Warsaw Pact members invaded the country to suppress the reformist movements.In October 1989, there were huge mass movement and strike happened and free elections and establishment of non-communist government by Vaclav Havel in December 1989, it led to the rejection of communist rule. In Romania in November 1989, violent mass movement and a civil war started that caused the dismissed of the communist government. In Bulgaria November 1989, nine independent organizations joined together to establish the Union of Democratic Forces, and in January 1990 that mounted the end of communist rule, and hence plural democracy and the market economy were adopted. So especially within two years of 1989-1990, these countries denounce communism and eventually fall of this regime in Eastern and Central Europe. So it was Endo-genetic (changes from within through mass resistance) for ideological and cultural change at large.

In this way, at the end of 1989, East Germany's communist leadership was forced from power due to the growing concern for democratization that swept through Eastern Europe. In November 1989, the East German government opened its border with West Germany and led to the fall of the Berlin Wall, and re-unification was made between East and West Germany. After that first openly-contested election was held for the new Congress of People's Deputy in Russia. In 1991, an open democratic election for the presidency and Boris Yeltsin resigned from the Russian communist party and became president of the Russian Soviet Federative Socialist Republic (not USSR). In August 1991, a revolt occurred by top communist leaders to re-build totalitarian USSR but all sorts of efforts were made failed within three days by the leadership of Boris Yeltsin. In late 1991, power was totally in the hands of Yeltsin. In September, Baltic Republics- Lithuania, Estonia, Latvia declared independence from USSR, and in November 1991, the Communist Party was banned in Russia. At last, 25 th December 1991 Gorbachev resigned and USSR formally dissolved.

Points to Remember

- Socialism is a system that shares economic output equally among all people. It beliefs the collective well-being of the community.
- Karl Marx and Friedrich Engels's book 'The Communist Manifesto' (1848) was written only before the Revolutions of 1848 swept Europe, manifesting scientific socialism.
- Rise of socialism in Eastern and Central Europe started after the Bolshevik revolution in 1917 to 1922, Russia became the first communist state.
- In the first half of the 20th century, the Soviet Union and the Communist parties of the third international arose around the world mainly to characterize socialism in terms of the Soviet model of economic development.
- After World War II, Russia allowed quasi-independent status to Eastern Europe nations as satellite and paramount power was on USSR and accordingly imposed communist regime in central as well as Eastern Europe.

Further Readings

A. Brown, 'The Idea of Communism', in *Rise and Fall of Communism*, Harpercollins (ebook), 2009, pp. 1-25;

R. Meek, 'The Definition of Socialism: A Comment', *The Economic Journal*, 1957, 67 (265), pp. 135- 139

Arye L. Hillman, "The transition from socialism: An overview from a political economy perspective", *European Journal of Political Economy*, 1994, Vol. 10, Issue 1, pp. 191-225.

Multiple Choice Questions

(a) Whose idea denotes –"From each according to his ability, to each according to his contribution."

(i) Capitalism (ii) Socialism

(iii) Communism (iv) Liberalism

(b) Who has written the book 'The Communist Manifesto'in 1848?

(i) Karl Marx and Friedrich Engels

(ii) Karl Duetch

(iii) Karl Marx

(iv) Ralph Miliband

(c) The history of socialism has its roots in –

(i) French Revolution (1789)

(ii) Russian Revolution (1917)

(iii) American Revolution (1775-1789)

(iv) Cuban Revolution (1979)

(d) When USSR was formally formed ?

(i) December 1922 (ii) September 1917

(iii) Febuary 1921 (iv) December 1920

(e) In 1947, Cominform (Communist Information Bureau) was formed by whom?

(i) Stalin (ii) Lenin

(iii) Marx (iv) Mao

(f) 'Glasnost' and 'Perestroika' are two structural reform initiatives introduced by which leader ?

(i) Mikhail Gorbachev (ii) Hitler

(iii) Mussolini (iv) Mao Zedong

(g) When didthe Berlin Wall fall ?

(i) Nov, 1989 (ii) Nov, 1991

(iii) March, 1989 (iv) January, 1990

Notes

1. Karl Marx. "*Critique of the Gothra Program*,"(United States: Wildside Press, 2008), Page 27.
2. McCormick, "*Communist and Post-Communist States in Comparative Politics in Transition*", (United Kingdom: Wadsworth, 2007), pp. 195-209.

Chapter - 5

Colonialism and De-Colonialization: Meaning, Context and Forms of Colonialism: Anti colonialism struggles and process of de-colonisation

Meaning of Colonialism

Colonialism is a policy or practice of acquiring full or partial political control over another country, occupying it with settlers, and exploiting it economically. It means the practice by which a powerful country directly controls less powerful countries and uses its resources to increase its power and wealth.It was a historical phenomenon of territorial expansion, is deeply connected with the rise and growth of the modern capitalist world-system. Thus, Colonialism is the extension of a nation's rule over territory beyond its borders. Colonizing countries usually control and exploit the resources, labour, and markets of the colonized. In this way, colonialism is a complex phenomenon of capitalist expansion. In a modern sense, colonialism refers to the process of control of supplies of raw materials, mineral resources, and markets in underdeveloped and pre-capitalist regions. However, such narrow definitions of colonialism overlook vital aspects of colonialism relating to political activity and the drive for dominance over the daily lives of the people of colonialism

In a modern sense, colonialism is a general description of the state of subjection-political, economic, and intellectual of a non-

European society as a result of the colonial organization. Thus, colonialism as a historical phenomenon refers to foreign domination which implies that the colonized area is regulated in a manner known as unequal exchange. Colonized societies are intended to serve the interests of the ruling country.

So, by colonialism, it means a system of political and social relations between two countries of which one is the ruler and the other is its colony. Thus, colonialism refers to foreign domination in society, economic and political policies of the colonial countries.

Basic features of Colonialism

One of the basic features of colonialism is that under it the colony is integrated into the world capitalist system in a subordinate position. It is characterized by an unequal exchange.

The exploitative international division of labor indicates that the monopolies produced goods of the high value with high technology and colonies produced goods of low value and productivity with low technology. The colony produced raw materials while the metropolis produced manufactured goods. The economic and social development of a colonial country is completely subordinated to the ruling country. The colonial economy takes all independent economic decisions.

Economic policies of colonies confirm to the interests of the rulers and not of the subjects. Hence, this unequal relationship between these countries results in a state of underdevelopment of the colony. India was the largest colonial possession of Britain, she was able to exploit India for nearly 200 years-1757-1947.

Colonialism is the establishment, maintenance, requisition, and expansion of colonies in one territory by people from another territory. Thus, colonialism is a relationship between an indigenous majority and a minority of foreign invaders for territorial expansion.

Difference between Colonialism and Imperialism

Though both the term are interrelated they have slightly different concepts. Colonialism derived from the Latin word 'colonia' which means settlement on foreign land. Whereas imperialism derives from the Latin word 'Imperium' that means order or command. It signifies power and authority of one country that also denotes at what extend a country can exercise its power and influence over other countries or territories. That indicates imperialism is a policy of extending the control and authority of one country over foreign territory. Usually, a country has two methods of implementing imperialism- indirect and direct method. When one country exerts influence or provides domination over another by not directly interfering with its territory is called the indirect method. The indirect method a powerful country captures the weak country and started its settlement there along with controlling the whole political or economic system. In this way, by using its imperial power that powerful country conquest and establishes its settlements and authority directly over the later. So it can be said that imperialism denotes a policy by which a powerful nation extend its power over another country and colonialism is a practical application of this policy. Here, it is noted that colonialism does not simply mean living in a foreign territory but it implies living and dominating or exploiting the resources ofthat local people and taking advantage over them with permanent settlement and total control over politically as well as economically. Thus, the practice of colonialism is driven by the ideology of imperialism and colonialism is one of the methods of imperialism. Lastly, all colonialism is imperialism, but all imperialism is not colonialism.

Forms of Colonialism

Based on the economic relationship between colonizer and colonized people there are several forms of colonialism:

Mercantile or trading colonialism

The first phase of development was dominated by commerce and trade that is known as 'Mercantile colonialism'. Trading companies were heavily involved in both production and trade. In mercantile capitalism, colonies existed for the benefit of the home country. Colonies could not sell their raw materials to other country but the home country and they are not allowed to manufacture anything for export[1].

Industrial or extractive Colonialism: It involved the expansion of overseas markets for European manufacturing goods and the oversees production of raw materials and food for European countries.

Finance or Investment Capitalism: Where colonies become a ground for investment by the Colonial power it is called finance or investment capitalism. It is a stage of capitalism in which economic and political domination is exercised by financial institutions rather than by industrial capitalists.

Planter Colonialism: Plantation was an early method of colonization where settlers went to establish a permanent or semi-permanent colonial base, for example for planting tobacco or cotton. Such plantations were also frequently intended to promote Western culture and Christianity among nearby indigenous people. For example, the Philippines, Africa, Malaysia are colonies for monoculture plant-like sugar, cotton, rubber.

Transport Colonialism: It denotes trading port or seaport that is an important route for world trade and to control this when colonies are made it is called transport colonialism. For example, US pressure on Japan to open ports to foreigners in 1854 was not about trade but rather transport. This type of colonialism includes hubs like the Azores, Hawai that became a supply depot during World War II. Transport colonialism does not refer to the displacement of native peoples, but it does have a great impact on local economies and cultures by creating contact zones.

Apart from this, based on Models of control, Colonialism has other types such as Direct and Indirect colonialism. Direct colonialism such as India, Indonesia, Algeria, Kenya, and indirect colonialism are China, Thailand, Japan as these countries are not directly occupied by any powerful country but many European powers put economic and political pressures on them.

Moreover, based on settlement and motives Colonialism can be categorized as-

Settler Colonialism: Here a large number of people from colonizing power settle down permanently to stay and cultivate in the colonized

land. It denotes large-scale immigration, often motivated by religious, political, or economic reasons. It intentions largely to replace any existing population. Here, a large number of people emigrate to the colony[2]. Australia, Canada, and the United States all exemplify settler-colonial societies[3].

Exploitative Colonialism

This type focuses on the exploitation of natural resources or population as labour, typically to the benefit of the colonial countries. It mainly refers to political subjugation and economic exploitation. This category refers to larger colonies that would constitute much of the political and economic administration. For example, most of the European colonies in Asia and Africa.

Surrogate Colonialism

Surrogate Colonialism involves a settlement project supported by a colonial power, in which most of the settlers do not come from the same ethnic group as the ruling power. It was coined by Scott Atran. It means colonizing power encourages and provides support for settling a non-native group over land occupied by indigenous people. Such as the British allowing Zionist settlement in Palestine.

Internal Colonialism

This type of colonialism was coined by Frantz Fanon. It denotes a notion of uneven structural power between areas of a state[4]. The source of exploitation comes from within the state. Internal colonialism thus means oppression and subordination of one group or region by another group or region in a decolonized country. For example, ethnic domination of Sinhalese in Sri Lanka, the racial oppression of Blacks in the USA by Whites.

De-colonialization

De-colonialization defines the withdrawal from its colonies of colonial power, the acquisition of political and economic independence by such colonies. It refers particularly in the years after World War II, of the colonial empires established before World War I throughout the world.

Decolonization not only refers to the complete removal of the domination of non-indigenous forces within the geographical sphere and different institutions of the colonized but also refers to the 'decolonization of the mind' from the colonizer that made the colonized feel inferior.Thus, decolonization represented not only the transference of legal sovereignty but also a movement for moral justice and political solidarity against imperialism.

The United Nations special committee on decolonization had stated that in the process of decolonization there is an alternative to the colonizer following a process of self- determination, but in practice, de-colonization may involve either non-violence, revolution or national liberation wars by pro-independence groups. Thus, decolonization is a political process and vital internationalization of the rejection of colonized mindsets and norms.So it can be said that de-colonization denoted denial of superiority of European culture and civilization and reclaiming the indigenous culture and civilization. Further, it refers to the anti-imperialist political movement and to an emancipatory ideology that sought to liberate the nation as well as humanity itself.

There are various causes of de-colonization-

The Atlantic charter was a document produced in 1941 that entailed the goals of the allied powers if they should win World War II. One of the provisions of that charter was that all people had the right to self- determination means all persons/nations had the right to govern themselves.

Decolonization after 1945 took place as a result of various factors- the colonized people just after the independence of World War II which demonstrated that colonial powers are no longer invulnerable and a new focus on anti-colonialism in international areas such as United Nations.

Another cause is development within the colonies and especially their development to modern societies. European colonialism as led to a westernized educated elite within the colonized countries and has led to the socio-economic and technological modernization as a whole. Western-educated elites spread the nationalized ideas into colonized nations that emerged as independence movements.

World War II was devastated by the economics of Western Europe and they probably did not enough money to continue to maintain empires. The formation of United Nations organizations played a major role in their context. The earlier state thought that small countries would not stand for their own decisions. After the creation of the UN that become foremost agency for decolonisation process and providea moral right for self government. Most of the African nations were not subjected to with the exploitation of economy done by the British. Most of the cash crops such as coffee, coca were sold under lower price and the mining profit also went to European share holders.

Apart from this, due to the weakened European powers after two world wars; rise of USA and USSR as superpowers with opposite ideologies; rise of Germany and Japan as new imperial power; setting up of UN and its role in giving voice to colonized nations; the anti-colonial struggle and nationalist movements in colonial nations; independence of India and other Africa- Asian nations against colonialism; the ideological crisis of post -World War I. As a result of these causes decolonization process started and it led to the independence of colonies mostly in Asia and African nations where people realized that they have the right to govern themselves. But these newly liberated countries faced some challenges like instability of the post-colonial political systems, economic problems, growing disparities between the northern and southern parts of the globe. Moreover, unlike the colonial time, now they were free and started to revive their old culture and religious & ethnic movements facilitated interactions of cultures. Also, few newly independent countries acquired stable governments immediately; others were ruled by dictators or military for decades or endured long civil wars.

Anti-Colonialism

D'souza defines anti-colonialism as the doctrine that rich countries of the West got rich by evolving, occupying poor countries of Asia, Africa, and South America. And even when former colonies secure political independence, anti-colonialist believe that they remain economically dependent on their former captors.

Anti-colonialism in South East Asia has been considered from a wide range of perspectives, resulting in deliberation over its character and place in the region's history. Generally, anti-colonialism refers to one type of Southeast Asian response to the encounter with Euro-American colonialism. Most especially, anti-colonialism has also come to represent how colonized people resisted, protested, or expressed or dissatisfaction imposed by colonial authorities. There are a variety of ways in which Southeast Asian countries respond to colonialism, it can be approached under three general catagories-

The first category of anti-colonialism represent those traditional movements that occurs as a reactions to the immediate military operations of the colonial powers. That proceeded the establishment of administrative government. These movements are generally led by elites in association with the vocabulary and symbols of leadership of pre-colonial authority. As these movements were based on villages and locally defined networks of relations, these outbreaks of resistance were limited in scale.

The second category of anti-colonialism includes those expressions that provide cooperation of indigenous and European ideals, refers generally to the types of programs initiated by educated indigenous elites who wanted to initiate change and reform through the colonial system adopted from European education. Those forms of the cottage were undertaken after colonial administrative and social institutions, producing a generation of social reforms that show the needs for the mechanism of the colonial system. This category sought to initiate social reform within the parameters of colonial law.

The third type of anti-colonial response which was more radical than the earlier attempts describes the initiatives of younger, educated urban students and activists who sought complete independence from colonial authorities using the organization and sometimes ideological blueprint of Japan and America. In contrast to the generation of educational elites who hope to initiate social reforms the leaders of these movements aimed to uproot the colonial powers using the language of anti-colonial nationalism to bridge the rural-urban gap by making the colonial experience at the common inspiration to launch the popular movement towards g independence.

These three categories of analysis take into account the socio-political changes that occurred within the South East Asian colonial society during the late 19th and the earlier twentieth society communities.

Processes and Struggles of decolonization

Decolonization refers to colonial rulers by the suppressed colonies. The struggle against colonial powers started due to the rise of nationalism in European countries. The nationalist ideas have a very strong impact in the colonies of Africa, Asia, and Latin America and that helped in began the anti-colonial movement in their respective territories of self-determination. These struggles eventually resulted in de-colonization which means freedom of colonies from imperial subjugation.

Decolonization refers to the achievements of independence by various western colonies and practices in Asia and Africa following World War II. De-colonization can be achieved by attaining independence integrating with administering power. It is a political process sometimes involving violence in extreme circumstances and maybe involves peaceful negotiations or violent revolt and arms struggle by the native population.Colonized people organized anti-colonial movements that asserted their rights to self-government. In this sense, nationalism gained momentum during the 20th century. Many believed that the staring of this thought process can be traced back to 1905 when Japan victory over Russia (a very powerful colonizing country that time)- the first victory of the dominated peoples against imperial power. This incident made other colonies realize about their liberation. Anti-colonial struggles intensified during the inter-war period especially between1918 to 1939 but not a coherent event like the Russian revolution or French revolution as this process continues to almost 25-30 years. This anti-colonial struggle was accompanied gradually by developing national consciousness in the colonies. The timings and patterns of decolonization were varied, and the purpose of the anti-colonial struggles in different colonies was not always consistent with each other. The only common pattern and process were that all were led by western-educated urban elites, great leaders successful in mass mobilization and inculcating national consciousness like Gandhi in India, unified resistance for political and cultural sovereignty, nation-building, the political process and institution-building on the pattern of European nation-states. Though the mass leaders were western educated and political process and institution-building were on the pattern of Europe, but the only change was that masses felt that it was owned and controlled by the masses. So some countries tried to root out the whole European system totally from their land but some other countries like India adopted that European pattern and structure after independence. However, the first country to get independence was the Philippines from the United States in 1946. But India's independence in 1947 accelerated the decolonization process first in Asia, then West Africa, and later on East Africa.

In 1955 Bandung conference was held in which newly independent Afro-Asian nation's denounced imperialism and expressed solidarity, further accelerated decolonizing in Asia and Africa. During that time the United Nations got its pace and also discussion was going on about the issue. The even USA and Russia two major power also denounce colonial policies. So along with that, the intensified liberation struggle also provides challenges to colonial powers. Moreover, in 1961 Non-Aligned Movement started were newly independent countries decided they were not joined in either power bloc of USA and USSR that also fuelled the decolonization process.

Apart from this, if we see the Marxist perspectives they observed that decolonization was a process of integration of the post-colonial state into a global capitalist system as a periphery or exploited region where the colonial country (core) exploit the resources- raw material or labour of colonies. According to them, decolonization was not led to independent states rather it was a development of underdevelopment described by Gunder Frank in his dependency theory. In this way, the decolonization process was expanded especially in Asia and Africa.

Points to remember

- It was a historical phenomenon of territorial expansion, is deeply connected with the rise and growth of the modern capitalist world-system.

- The colony produced raw materials while the metropolis produced manufactured goods. The economic and social development of a colonial country is completely subordinated to the ruling country.
- Direct colonialism such as India, Indonesia, Algeria, Kenya, and indirect colonialism are China, Thailand, Japan as these countries are not directly occupied by any powerful country but many European powers put economic and political pressures on them.
- De-Colonialisation refers particularly in the years after World War II, of the colonial empires established before World War I throughout the world.
- Colonized people organized anti-colonial movements that asserted their rights to self-government.

Further Reading

R. Suresh, "*Economy & Society -Evolution of Capitalism*", (New Delhi, Sage Publications, 2010) pp. 151-188; 235-268.

M. Dobb, "*Capitalism, in Studies in the Development of Capitalism*". (London: Routledge and Kegan Paul Ltd, 1950), pp. 1-32.

E. Wood, "*The Agrarian origin of Capitalism', in Origin of Capitalism: A Long View.*"(London: Verso, 2002), pp. 91-95; 166-181.

Multiple Choice Questions

(a) When did the Bandung Conference take place?

(i) 1954 (ii) 1955

(iii) 1956 (iv) 1960

(b) When did Non-Aligned Movement start?

(i) 1971 (ii) 1971

(iii) 1991 (iv) 1954

(c) When the process of de-colonization started?

(i) After World War I (ii) After World War II

(iii) Post- Cold War (iv) After French Revolution

(d) Decolonization is-

(i) A tactical maneuver.

(ii) The breaking of ties with the Mother Country.

(iii) A block of prison quarters.

(iv) None of the above

(e) What economic setback did Latin American countries experience after independence?

(i) A decrease in imports from foreign nations.

(ii) A lack of industrialization.

(iii) An increase in infrastructure, such as roads, railroads, and schools.

(iv) An increase in trade with foreign nations.

(f) Which was the first country to get independence from the United States in 1946?

(i) Philippines (ii) Palestine

(iii) India (iv) South Korea

(g) Who coined the term 'Internal Colonialism'

(i) Frantz Fanon (ii) Scott Atran

(iii) Ander Gunder Frank (iv) Samir Amin

(h) In which year the Atlantic Charter was singed ?

(i) 1941 (ii) 1943

(iii) 1945 (iv) 1939

Notes

1. A. Hoogvelt, *"History of Capitalism Expansion, in Globalization and Third World Politics"*, (London: Palgrave, 2002), pp. 14-28.

2. Barker, Adam J, "The Contemporary Reality of Canadian Imperialism: Settler Colonialism and the Hybrid Colonial State". *American Indian Quarterly*, 2009, 33 (3): 325-351.

3. Gabbidon, Shaun, "*Race, Ethnicity, Crime, and Justice: An International Dilemma*", (Los Angeles, CA: SAGE, 2010). p. 8.

Unit - III

Themes for Comparative Analysis

Chapter - 6

Comparative Study of Constitutional Development and Political economy of the following countries: Britain, China, Brazil and Nigeria

Constitutional Development of Britain

Great Britain has the unique distinction of having a very long and continuously developing history of evolution of democratic institutions. The British Constitutions which is an unwritten Constitutions working through a large number of well recognized political traditions.

Origin and Evolution of Monarchy

Monarchy has been the oldest political institutions of England. During the 600 AD to 1066 AD the monarchy was absolute. But in practice all powers are exercised with the advice of a council, which was known as Witenagemot or the Council of the Wise. Kingship was hereditary as well as elective. In 1066, England was conquered by William of Normandy and he brought about several big changes in the constitutional system. He distributed the land among his tenants-in-chief & tenants and assigned to them several responsibilities. One of their responsibilities was to sit in the meetings of kings Great Council- the Magnum Concilium. It helped the king in running the administration. Thus Great Council replaced the Witenagemot.

Later out of the Great Council a small body, the Royal Council was constituted and the king exercised all the powers with the help of both. The Monarchy began acting as a strong and absolute Monarchy. This strong Monarchy however transformed into a despotic monarchy up to 1135. This made the development of big feudal lords-the Barons. Later, the Barons got united to compel the King to accept certain rules and limitations. It led to the development of Magna Carta that later became law.

The Magna Carta, 1215

Magna Carta came to be the first historical charter which placed some limitations upon the exercise of powers by the king. It laid the foundations for the emergence of a limited monarchy in England. Under it, the King can lavy any tax without common consent; the king cannot deny or delay the grant of justice to his people. The emergence of the rule of the Tudor kings (1485-1603) led to the establishment of a strong Monarchy acting in and absolute manner but without becoming despotic, a royal organized and active parliament with an efficient Privy council and a network of courts.

However, the strong centralized monarchy established by the Tudors was sought to be converted into an arbitrary system of governance by James and Charles I (1603-1649). This led to the struggle for supremacy between the parliament and the King. However, the Monarchy abolished between 1649-60. In this year, England continued to be a commonwealth under a written constitution. In 1660, Commonwealth failed and parliament was restored. It led to the Glorious Revolution in 1688 that confirmed the establishment of the Supremacy of the British parliament. In 1680 the Bill of Rights was passed which placed legal restrictions upon the powers of the King. In the 18th century, England experienced the emergence of the cabinet system and the office of the Prime Minister.

Origin and Evolution of the British Parliament

The British Parliament is the oldest in the world. It can be traced back to the Witenagemot of Anglo Saxon (600 AD- 1066) or the Magnum Concilium (Great Council). Initially, the parliament acted as a common meeting place for the three groups of representatives of Barons, Clergy, and Commonality. However, in the 14th century, a division took place among the Barons when higher Barons and lower Barons formed two separate groups. The higher Barons joined hands with the Clergy. That formed the House of Lords and the small Barons join hands with the commonality to form the House of commons. In this way, by the end of the 14th century, a bi-cameral well established Parliament discharging the functions of law-making, granting of finances and advising the monarch.

Political Economy of Britain

Political Economy generally defines the interaction between politics and economics and how they affect each other. It further seeks to understand how history, culture, and politics impact an economic system. If we talk about the political economy of Britain it can be prominent in some phases.

Before World War II

In the medieval period, feudal society prevailed (like the Zamindary system in India) and the economy was agrarian. In the 15th & 16th centuries, there was an evolution of large scale commercial farming and market-based economy led to the emergence of the capitalist agrarian economy. Britain was one of the most prosperous economic regions in Europe between 1600 and 1700. In the 17th century mercantile capitalism developed that led to monopoly trading companies and colonized several countries. However, from the middle of eighteenth-century Industrialisation (various manufacturing industries steam engines, textile equipment, railway system, etc.) took place in the UK that gave rise to economic developments gradually and industrial capitalism evolved that raw materials exploited from colonies. These resulted in Britain becoming one of the premier economies in Europe during the first half of the 19th century, the most prominent industrial power in the world economy, and a major political entity. After 1840, an economic policy of mercantilism was restrained and replaced it by "free trade," with few tariffs or restrictions. The powerful Royal Navy tried for prospering British interests, shipping, and international trade, at the same time, the British legal system carried a system for resolving disputes quite economically, and the City of London acted as the economic capital and focus of the world economy.

Between 1945-1970s

After World War II, in 1945 Labour Party led by Clement Attlee got the enormous victory and introduced massive reform of the economy as Britain's economy got deteriorated and national re-construction need was felt. So large political consensus began for how to deal with the new circumstances and assured for the state to play an interventionist and welfare role in every aspect. For example, the state shall have a primary role in economic management, education, health care, social security, maintain a healthy rate of growth and nation-building, etc. The nationalization of major sectors took place. In this way, after 15 years of the rapid growth experienced in Britain. In early 1957 Harold Macmillan came to power and by 1959, tax reduction had helped augmentation of living standards and maintain a strong economy. In this way, the economy remained strong, and having a low unemployment rate in the 1960s but gradually towards the later years it witnessed slow growth. In 1970, the Labour leader voted out of power and Edward Heath of Conservative Party ruled, But by the 1970s the manufacturing sector gradually declines its share both at domestic as well as international levels. Moreover, the economic crisis emerged due to economic degradation, a rise in inflation, frequent strikes social instability, etc. Apart from this, with neither the Conservative government of 1970-1974 led by Edward Heath) nor the Labour government that succeeded it (led by Harold Wilson and from 1970 James Callaghan) can combat the economic decline and winter of discontent(during 1978-79 widespread strikes by public sector trade unions) finally marked the end of Golden era of Britain.

The era of Neo-liberalism –Thatcher Era

In 1979, Margaret Thatcher succeeded Edward Heath from the Conservative Party and initiated a series of economic policies to overcome the situation. In this way, her political idea and economic strategies underlined on flexible labour markets, the minimal intervention of the state in market economy approved the privatization of state-regulated companies (of some sections), promote entrepreneurship, individual autonomy,reform in tax, a decrease of power and influence of trade unions. Thus, as a result of these changes showed significant growth in GDP, inflation decreased, low rate of unemployment, etc. But in the long run, it did not maintain. By 1989, the rate of economic growth slowed down, unemployment and interest rates increased.

In November 1990, John Major was elected as the successor of Thatcher. During that time, the massive recession began and it was probably the longest recession since the Great Depression. Up to 1993, 3 million people were unemployed. As British pound was tied to EU exchange rates due to the part of the Exchange Rate Mechanism (ERM) that steered to the adversity for Britain. It also heavily challenged the Conservative party's agenda for economic strategies and marked the 18 years of this government in 1997.

1997-2010: New Labour Era

The Labour Party that has a socialist agenda since its inception, undergo some change under the leadership of Tony Blair and Gordon Brown and this New Labour criticized for traditional socialist policies. It was emphasized on both the ideology of socialism and capitalism- a kind of mixed economy for Britain that would help for overall development adopted the best of the market economy. This party mainly focused on providing social justice, equality of opportunity, had faith in the use of markets to bring economic efficiency and modernization.Gradually also accepted Globalisation- preferring FDI, control of inflation, effective training to participate in the global labour market for proper economic administration, make provisions for social welfare, etc. In 1997, his government gave the Bank of England powers to set interest rates and caused a large increase in public spending. He championed multiculturalism and between 1997 and 2007, immigration rose tremendously when the government welcomed immigration New EU member states in 2004 that led to cheap labor supply. He introduced the National Minimum Wage Act, 1998, Human Rights Act 1998, Freedom of Information Act, 2000. But he got criticized among public during the War on Terror for guaranteeing that British Armed Forces participated in the War in Afghanistan in 2001 and 2003 invasion of Iraq. In 2005 did win but the reduced majority. During that time, the UK continues to lose a large number of manufacturing jobs, and later in 2008 the UK entered a recession, and the unemployment rate has risen. In 2007 Blair officially resigned in the late 2009 recession ended. In 2010, the first time in England Conservative (David Cameron) and Labour Party (Nick Clegg) formed a full coalition government since World War II. While Cameron became PM and Clegg became Deputy Prime Minister. In May 2015 elections several minor parties stood along with the major parties in Great Britain were the Conservatives, Labour and Liberal Democrats. The First Past the Post system continues to fail the British electorate. It was the most disproportional election that reflected the most disproportionate result in UK history, millions voted for smaller parties, a majority Conservative government gained less than 37% of the vote and with the support of just 24% of the electorate.Labours though saw their vote increase but the number of seats collapsed. At the same time, Conservatives won with the majority but got a minority number of vote share and Liberal Democrats lost nearly all their seats despite getting 8% of the total vote. UK's voting system- The First Past The Post System was in crisis as masses criticize this system as outdated and unfit to multiparty period. In 2016, after Cameron resigned, Theresa May elected as Conservative Party leader. The British economy's growth slowed down and at the same time referendum on withdrawing from the European Union (Brexit) took place. The British voters who supported leaving the EU were 51.9% against 48.1% to remain with the EU. Britain wanted to exit because the basic problem is associated with immigration policy, resources can be used by all as there is no boundary line. So Britain wants to stay away from this, unemployment problem raises, use of job, resource from another country could also possible. Actually as a result all countries are interdependent n dependent. On 27 March 2017 Teresa execute article 50 of Lisbon Treaty, officially want to exit from the EU. There is a rule that after the decision to exit from the EU, Britain has 2 years from the execution of article 50 and has to decide the terms and conditions of how to exit. But the major problem was the 'Deal Or No Deal' issue. If no deal is there Britain became like India, Sri Lanka, and no longer a part of the EU- as Britain's economy is based on EU (no tax, no tariff is needed if Britain wants to sell a product to countries of EU). But if exit varies countries vary taxes are there and would have faced lots of financial problems. Taxes have to pay and have to face competition. In July 2019, Boris Johnson took over as Prime Minister. Later, on 31st January 2020 UK formally left the EU. UK has agreed on the terms of its EU departure but both sides must concern about their future relationship. Britain is now a transitional period till 31st December 2020 during which makes the UK bound to the EU's rules. However, the transition also indicates the UK will continue to contribute to the EU's budget.

Constitutional Development of China

The Communist Party of China was founded in 1921, during the May Four Movement. Mao Zedong referred to as the birth of communism in China. After a period of slow growth and alliance with the Kuomintang (Chinese Nationalist Party), the alliance collapsed and the Communists fell victim in 1927 to the condition carried out by the Kuomintang under the leadership of Chiang Kai-shek. After 1927, the Communists withdrew to the countryside and built up local bases throughout the country and continued to hold them until the Long March. Since the establishment of the People's Republic of China in 1949, the Long March has been considered as an example of the Communist Party's strength and spirit. It resulted in the relocation of the communist revolutionary base from southern-eastern to north-western China and in the emergence of Mao Zedong as the undisputed party leader. After the Chinese Civil War 1945-49 resulted in a decisive Communist victory. On October 1, 1949, Mao Zedong officially proclaimed the founding of the People's Republic of China.

Constitutionalism between1949-54

After that, the communists did not base their government on any constitution. They decided to hold for a formulated constitution and wanted to rely upon Mao's leadership and People's Democratic Dictatorship as guided by him. During that time, a Chinese People's

Political Consultative Conference was organized representing all political groups and mass organizations that signified to legalize the system created for carrying out Mao's Common Programme. The Organic Law was promulgated consisting of 31 Articles and it delineated the structure and functions of the governmental machinery and had been entrusted with the responsibility of fulfilling the common program. The arrangement continued till 1954.

Constitutionalism between 1954-75

It was in 1953 that the People's Republic of China decided to have a written constitution. A committee under the chairmanship of Mao Tse-tung was created for this purpose. This committee proposed the draft of a constitution which was submitted to the people of China and their organizations for a full national debate. The Chinese People's Government incorporated several amendments in the draft for incorporating the views of the people. The amended draft was presented to the National People's Political Conference in September 1954. After its adoption, the Constitution led to the formation of a new government on 4th November 1954. The 1954-Constitution affirmed the resolve of the people of China to overthrow colonialism, feudalism, and capitalism. The Preamble and Article 19 of the Constitution acclaimed the vital role of the Communist Party in achieving revolution against imperialism and exploitation but did not give it a constitutional recognition. The Constitution, further, accepted the principle of democratic centralism and expressed the resolve to safeguard the people's democratic system. Through this Constitution, the Chinese accepted the concept of granting fundamental rights and duties to the citizens. It recognized seven fundamental freedoms of the citizens, their social, economic and political rights, and duties towards the socialists. While abandoning capitalism, it recognized the right to private property of the citizens. Indeed, the theory of constitutionalism written in this constitution was however never really followed in actual practice.

The Cultural Revolution that was initiated by Mao after the failure of the Great Leap Forward (1958), produced several big turmoils in the Chinese society and political system. It was designed to reform the people by making them true socialists-both in thought and action. Mao's Red Guards, the committed soldiers of the Cultural Revolution, became active in eliminating capitalism. But in actual practice, however, the Cultural Revolution resulted in violence and destabilization. Further, it flashed the struggle between Mao and the Liu Shao-Chi factions. The Army also came to assert its role by organizing new revolutionary committees. By 1969, China had to dismiss the Cultural Revolution in favor of a new struggle for achieving socialist goals. It, however, resulted in the defeat of Liu Shao-Chi faction. Mao and his loyalists continued to be most powerful. After Mao's death, the leftists, the Shanghai group-'the Gang of Four' led by Mao's wife Chiang Ching fell into the background. This led to the formal end of the era of the Cultural Revolution, however, came in 1975, when a new constitution was adopted and implemented in China.

The Constitution of 1975 and Chinese Constitutionalism

Constitutionalism in China recorded a change in 1975 under the impact of the results of the Cultural Revolution. Further, this change was considered essential because the 1954 Constitution had been formulated for a transitional period of 20 years. However, it consisted of only 30 Articles divided into only 4 chapters and had a very long Preamble. The Preamble narrated the past achievements of China during 1954-75.

The Preamble of the 1975-Constitution called upon the people of China to follow the policies of the Communist Party, maintain continued revolution, and consolidate the unity of the people of all nationalities based on the alliance of workers and peasants, and develop the revolutionary front. In these constitutions, the National People's Congress was defined as the highest organ of state power under the leadership of the Communist party. It abolished the office of the Chairman of the Republic and vested the powers of the head of the State in the Standing Committee of the National People's Congress. It maintained the list of the Fundamental Rights and Freedoms of the citizens with some improvements. It gave the right to freedom of procession and freedom of strike to the people. It curtailed the list of duties.

The Constitution of 1978

Constitutionalism under the influence of Hua Guo-Feng

The 1975-Constitution had a short life of three years. The death of Mao Tse-tung in 1976 and the ensuing power struggle within the hierarchy of the Communist Party brought into prominence the leadership of Hua Guo-Feng. This struggle for power gave rise to the need for a new constitution.

The 1978 Constitution made several major changes in the 1975 constitution. Its stated objective was: "The Consolidation of the socialist economic base" and "development of the productive forces at high speed." It accepted "Socialist Democracy as the goal which was to be achieved by arousing the socialist enthusiasm of the people of all our nationalities to strive for the fulfillment of the central task for the new period."

The constitution gave recognition to the role of the army by providing that the Chinese Liberation Army is the workers' and peasants' armed force led by the Communist Party. "It was the pillar of the dictatorship of the Proletariat." The 1978 Constitution further extended the list of Fundamental Rights and Freedoms of the Chinese and now it came to include the right to "speak out freely, air the views fully and hold great debates. It guaranteed a socialist democratic system with a unicameral National People's Congress (NPC) as the highest organ of state power.

NPC was given the power to choose the Premier acting upon the recommendation of the Central Committee of the Communist Party. The members of its State Council were to be appointed by the NPC upon the recommendations of its Standing Committee.

The powers of the NPC were to be exercised by its Standing Committee during the interval between its two sessions. The State Council was made responsible before the NPC, and during its absence, it was to be responsible before the Standing Committee of the NPC. The 1978-Constitution expressed full faith in the ideology of Marxism-Leninism and Mao Tse-Tung's thought. It reflected in article 16 of the Constitution prescribed that all the personnel of the state should study Marxism-Leninism-Maoism. Apart from this, the 1978 Constitution accepted fully the principal role of the Communist Party. The Central Committee of the Communist Party has ascertained the main role in determining the choice of high ranking officers of the state including the Premier. The Chairman of the Central Committee of the party was to command the armed forces. Therefore, the Communist Party continued to be the crucial instrument of the Chinese Political System.

The Constitution of 1982: New Constitutionalism

The power struggle within the Communist Party that had arisen after the death of Mao, brought another drastic change in the Chinese leadership and accordingly in Chinese Constitutionalism. By 1981, Hua Guo-Feng lost power and Deng Xiaoping emerged as the strongman along with General Secretary Zhao ZhLang. The new leadership then provide a new constitution to China with several liberalizing changes. Under the constitution, the concentration of powers in individual hands was curtailed and the concept of collective leadership was accepted and the need to give due share to the younger generation leadership was recognized. A new emphasis on decentralization and liberalization of the economy. The private sector in China's socialist economy was assigned a role. China decided to go in for a 'multi-faceted economy', including **"Joint Socialist Private Enterprises"**, came to be an accepted new principle of the Chinese economy and more openness in Chinese politicsThus, the 1982 Constitution accepted Marxism-Leninism-Maoism but along with it, a new need for liberalization, decentralization, modernization and market socialism was accepted. It secured a separation between the Government and the Party. In this way, it tried to give a new orientation to the Chinese Political Culture. Thus, the Constitution of 1982 and the features it incorporated continue to guide the activities and policies of the People's Republic of China in this 21st century.

Political Economy of China

After 1948 when the People's Republic of China was established in 1949, almost the majority of people lived in rural areas and agriculture occupied 65% of national income. Under the leadership of Mao, who advocated for a diversified industrial structure through a system of central planning ideas influenced by the Soviet system. Between 1949-1978 marked by a clash over economic and social policy. Due to major importance on the socialist scheme, rural and urban incomes were stagnant before two decades of reform. As much concern was provided on economic growth that was followed by substantial levels of capital accumulation. This resulted in using resources mostly on these areas rather than much emphasis on improving popular living standards. In this way, due to the failure of the Soviet kind of industrialization of China that emphasized capital accumulation from the surplus agricultural product which was not possible because of the large number of population.

So to cope up with the situation an experimental commune was established in 1958 that assured that both agro-industrial could be lifted by altering the mass's working habits and much emphasis on diversification of labour rather than machine oriented industrial procedures. Under this system, decentralisation process was followed in agricultural and political decisions. But it did not work and during 1958-60 approximately 30 million people died due to massive hunger[1]. This caused degradation of the Chinese economy. So the government revoked the Great Leap Forward Program and communal system withered. This failure resulted in a division among the party leaders.

In 1966 under Mao Zedong's leadership a young group of Red Guards formed to challenge party officials and to attack the bourgeoisie launched Cultural Revolution, a socio-political movement to reestablish Mao's political ideology in Chinese Communist Party. Its basic aim was to destroy the "four olds" - old ideas, old customs, old habits and old culture" and to revive and inculcate revolutionary principles in the younger generation. Schools and universities were closed. In October 1966, Mao ordered Red Guards to destroy these four olds. In January 1967, Red Guard overthrew the provincial party committee officials and got substituted by radicals. In July the same year, the Red Guard confronted the political leadership at Wuhan and the City administration tried to resist them that led to total civil war.So the chaotic situation continued and huge losses of life and economy took place. In late 1968 Mao realized this revolution got soared and to restrain violence he ordered to re-educate the youth and also asked the army to restore order and efficiently transforming China into a military dictatorship that continued until 1971. In between 1971 cultural revolution ended. However, the cultural revolution officially ended after Mao's death in September 1976.

So after his death increasing inefficiency had marked a drastic change in the political economy of China in 1978 from a centrally planned system to a market-oriented economy. Accordingly, its economic growth had been lifted and poverty got reduced. The reforms include price reform, state-owned enterprise (SOE) reform, granting market access to the private sector, etc. Moreover, economic control of various enterprises was given to provincial and local governments, which were generally allowed to operate and compete on free-market principles, rather than under the direction and guidance of state planning. Further, from 1984 to 1994 price reform took place, and after that SOE reform continued for a longer time. The private sector along with state-owned enterprises massively contributing China's economic strength. This reform got its peak after China acceded to the World Trade Organisation. In this way, the 1980s was concerned mainly with foreign investment. But again China's economic growth decelerated significantly aftermath of the Tiananmen massacre that happened in June 1989. Many nations including the United States impart trade sanctions against China. As a result, China's real GDP growth rate fell from 11.3% in 1988 to 4.2% in 1989 and declined to 3.9% in 1990[2]. In 1991, economic reforms were restarted and foreign sanctions against China were reduced or removed, and real GDP grew by 9.2%, and after 2000s opening was focused on 'going abroad.'[3] So after the reform, China's economic growth was significant. But its real GDP growth has slowed significantly, from 14.2% in 2007 to 6.6% in 2018, and that growth is projected by the International Monetary Fund (IMF) to fall to 5.5% by 2024.

The Chinese government indeed consider it as the "new normal" and admitting the requirement for China to adopt a fresh growth model that be dependent less on fixed investment and exporting, and basically on private consumption, services, and innovation to uplift economic growth. Such restructurings are desirable for China to elude the "middle-income trap," when countries attain a certain economic level but start to experience sharply lessening economic growth rates because they are incapable to take on new sources of economic growth like innovation. It has become a prime aim in its economic planning through a variety of initiatives for example "Made in China 2025," a plan declared in 2015 to update China's manufacturing in 10 fundamental sectors through wide-ranging government aid to establish China a major global player in respective sectors. However, such initiatives have taken to lessen the country's dependence on foreign tools and eventually dominate global markets.

Moreover, in2013 China's Belt and Road initiative (BRI) that was also known as "One Belt, One Road" initiated to lift economic integration and connectivity -infrastructure, trade, and investment with its neighbours and various trading partners in Asia, Africa, Europe, and the Middle East, etc. India did not join it due to the security concern about the China-Pakistan Economic Corridor (CPEC) considering violating its territorial sovereignty.

In 2017, the USA launched a Section 301 inquiry of China's innovation and intellectual property policies considered harmful to U.S. economic securities. In 2018 July, due to unfair trade practices, the USA consequently raised tariffs by 25% on $250 billion imports from China, while China increased tariffs (from 5% to 25%) on $110 billion worth of imports from the United States. Such measures have suddenly decreased bilateral trade in 2019. On May 10, 2019, President Trump said he admitted raising tariffs on nearly all remaining products from China. This escalating trade conflict between the United States and China could have negative consequences for the Chinese economy. On June 29, 2019, in the G 20 Osaka Summit Trump announces both countries agreed to a "truce" in the trade war after comprehensive talks. Though earlier tariffs are to remain in effect, no future tariffs are to be imposed "for the time being" amid restarted negotiations. Furthermore, Trump said he would permit American companies to sell their products to Huawei, but the company would continue on the U.S. trade blacklist. By May 2020 both relations had worsened as both sides were engaging allies to attack the other regarding guilt for the worldwide COVID-19 pandemic[4]. Relations worsened over the Chinese government's decision to authorize a Hong Kong national security law in 2020[5].

So, in 2020, China's economy is viewing some uncertain signs of recovery from the destruction caused by the novel coronavirus pandemic but the pathway remains hugely uncertain in 2020, putting millions of jobs at risk. GDP growth this year in the world's second-biggest economy could drop to just 1% or 2%, down from 6.1% in 2019, according to recent estimates by analysts[6]. Even the World Bank warned that in the worst scenario, the $14 trillion economy may not grow at all.

Constitutional Development of Brazil

1824 Constitution

Before 1822, Brazil was a colony of Portugal. In the same year Dom Pedro I declare himself independent and established a constitutional monarchy. It was by 1823, Emperor Pedro I started the political process of writing a Constitution. So before Brazil's independence on September 7th, 1822, there was no formal constitution. Since then, the country wrote seven other constitutions beginning with the constitution of 1824. The 1824 Constitution gave the Emperor extensive control over governing institutions, such as the legislature and provincial governments, and continued until 1889, when Pedro II was overthrown and landowning elites establish the oligarchical Republic of Brazil.

1891 Constitution (Old Republic)

This first republican constitution was established with a directly elected president. It established a presidential system and male universal suffrage from the age of 21. It contained provisions for separation of powers, checks, and balances, a bicameral legislature, direct elections, and created a Federal Chamber. Its former provinces were declared as States.

1934 - 1937 Constitutions(Era of New Republic)

In 1930, Getulio Vargas organized a military revolt. His government created a new Constitution in 1934. After some years, Vargas met a counter-revolution, forcing him to stage a coup, after which he initiated a new constitutional process. The resulting 1937 Constitution was authoritarian, concentrating executive and legislative powers in the President, who was the supreme authority of the State, elected by indirect elections for a term of six years. During that time, nationalism, social welfare, industrialization took place. The President had powers to appoint the Governors of the provinces, who in turn appointed the mayors of cities. As this was a de facto rule, Vargas legislated by decree. But during this period all political parties were dissolved and individual rights and guarantees were suspended. The government had a great intervention in the economy. The 1937 Constitution allowed Vargas to announce a dictatorship called the New State and to remain in power for another decade.

The 1946 Constitution

The 1946 Constitution replaced the New State's dictatorship of Getulio Vargas after he was overthrown by his war minister. Representative democracy was recognized and a new President, Eurico Gaspar Dutra, was elected for the next five years. An extensive franchise was granted. This constitution restores all rights and freedoms as expressed by the 1934 Constitution which had been suppressed in 1937. A constituent assembly drafted a more balanced and liberal Constitution that tried to re-established basic individual rights and the separation of powers. It also maintained an important role of the state in the nation's economy and reflected the inspiration of the U.S. Constitution concerning federalism

1967 Constitution and 1969 Constitution

After the military coup, 1964 the controllers promised to restore democracy as soon as possible. However, in due course, they did not and were faced with a problem, as every major initiative they took was firmly against that current constitution, including the coup itself. The Institutional Acts issued by the military presidents were given much importance than the constitution that could even amend it. In this crucial situation, the first military president tried to revitalize the civilian rule. But military and civilian extremists sensed that the military had to stay in power for some years. By 1965 these circumstances got deteriorated and all felt that the 1946 constitution was outdated and a new constitution was needed. Subsequently, the 1946 Constitution suffered many amendments through Institutional Acts which severely compromised its democratic character. It was replaced by a new constitution in 1967. This document was again changed through a constitutional reform in 1969. Both constitutions were characterized by centralized power in the executive, in particular in the President, as they sought to institutionalize the military regime. The presidential term of office was increased from four to five years, and the President was given more power to decree laws related to taxation, creation of public employment, and the determination of salaries for civil servants. This constitution characterized by restriction of political and civil rights, Military State Police Corps recognized as reserve corps of the Federal Army, entrusted with the undertaking of "providing public security", thereby reducing the autonomy of the existing civilian police. Moreover, after formerly disbanding of all political parties, new rules were written on the formation of parties. Bring about a series of controls, commissions to regulate several aspects of civil, social, and economic life, thus escalating an already existing trend towards bureaucracy, management of the economy by the central government as well. In 1969, this strictly authoritarian document was widely amended by the 1969 Amendment is sometimes regarded as a seventh Constitution, because it almost completely rewrote the text of the 1967 document. The new constitutional brought some extra implementation for the regime - providing the president the right to declare a state of emergency and suspend constitutional freedoms, Suspension of habeas corpus, special military courts, transfer of command of the military police from each federal state to the Ministry of the Army, etc.

The transition to the 1988 Constitution (Seventh Constitution)

In the 1970s, the military regime faced popular uprisings and dissatisfaction as economic progress began to slow. The transition from authoritarian rule to democracy started in 1974, however, the constitution was gradually terminated of its authoritarian character.

Accordingly, this process accelerated with the reoccurrence of civilian rule in 1985 and led to the adoption of a new constitution in 1988. The process started when President Ernesto Geisel and his Chief of Cabinet, General Golbery de Couto e Silva conducted a gradual process of political liberalization that was characterized by the creation of full democracy. The first important attempt was the organization of free congressional elections in 1974. In 1982 the military allowed direct elections for state governors and gradually increased federal transfers to municipal governments. Additionally, a new law was inaugurated on political parties resulting in an opening of political life. In 1985, the government approved the National Constituent Assembly for the drafting of a new constitution. In this process of drafting, participatory methodology and organized public hearings are followed. After twenty months of deliberation, the NCA created the 1988 "citizen constitution." Under the current Constitution, Brazil is a presidential, federal republic. Through an amendment in 1996, municipalities were incorporated with states as part of the federation. Consequently, the country is composed of 26 states and one Federal District (Brasilia). The federal, state, and municipal governments have their own legislative, executive, and judicial institutions.

In this way, the 1988 constitution has enormous value. As Luis Roberto Barroto has outlined that "the constitution symbolizes the culmination of the process of restoration of democracy under rule of law and the suspending of the authoritarian system characterized by tolerance, monopolization of power and violence."[7]

Political Economy of Brazil

Brazil is a federal and constitutional republic and the largest country in South America and Latin America. It comprised of 26 states and the Federal District. They have their constitution. These states are led by a governor and a chamber of state deputies but these are not that powerful compare to those in the federal government. The federal government consists of the Upper House, which is the Senate, and also the Camara Federal-united, they are also known as the Congress in Brazil. The President of Brazil is the head of state as well as the head of government of Union and he got elected every 4 years and can re-elect for the second term. It is also one of the most multicultural and ethnically diverse countries due to mass immigration from around the world.

Brazil is having a massive source of natural resources and is categorized as an upper-middle-income economy by the World Bank and an emerging industrialized country with the largest share of global wealth in Latin America.It has a developing free-market economy, the 9th largest in the world in 2019. Brazil is one of the world-leading producers of mining, agriculture, and manufacturing, and it has a strong and speedily growing service sector. It is a giant of a host of minerals such as iron ore, tin, bauxite, manganese, gold, quartz, and diamonds, etc. and it exports vast quantities of steel, automobiles, electronics, and consumer goods. Brazil is the world's major reservoir of coffee, oranges, and a key manufacturer of sugar, soy, etc. It can be noted that the absolute prominence of Brazilian agriculture has been diminishing since the mid-20th century when the planned to rapidly urbanize and massively exploit its mineral, industrial, and hydroelectric potential. Significantly, Sao Paulo city has become one of the world's major centers of commerce, finance, arts, and entertainment.

From the 16th to the mid-20th century, the country's export was mainly concentrated on a few agricultural products. At the prior stage of colonial times, the export of Brazil wood took place, and the 18th century dominated with the export of sugar and mineral-gold and diamond; coffee became a massive source of income from the mid-19th century, and rubber in the late 19th and early 20th centuries. In this way, in the 20th century, the Brazilian government endeavored to expand the country's production and lessen its reliance on agricultural exports by intensely boosting manufacturing.

From 2000 to 2012, Brazil was one of the fastest-growing major economies in the World. In the year 2004, Brazil's economy has shown a promising growth of 5.7% in GDP. As per the World Economic Forum, Brazil was the top country in the upward evolution of competitiveness in 2009.Brazil is a member of various economic organizations such as Mercosur, UNASUR, BRICS, G8+5, G 20, WTO, Paris Club, Cairns Group, etc.

Brazil's economic growth slowed down in 2013 and the country went into a recession in 2014. There was a tremendous reduction in economic activity in 2015 and 2016, with GDP falling by 3.6% and 3.4 % respectively. The economic crisis raised due to the dropping of commodity prices and the inability of the administration to take up necessary fiscal reforms.The economy underway however to revive in 2017 with GDP 1.1%. As a result of a number of reasons like weak labour market, investments overdue by uncertainties of elections, and trucker's general strike caused economic activities stagnant in 2018. Thus, re-establishing fiscal sustainability is a major economic challenge for Brazil and to cope with the situation a constitutional amendment (95/ 2016) was done to limit the rise of public spending. This imposes a fiscal adjustment of 4.1 % of GDP through 2026 and stabilizes the debt at about 81.7% of GDP in 2023. Executing this fiscal adjustment necessitates decreasing the rigidity of public spending and revenue allocating mechanism. But 2020 showed a devasted effect due to Coronavirus Pandemic and its related measures, Brazil's GDP dropping to -4.7% than the prior estimate growth of zero, which is the biggest annual fall since 1900. It manifested in growing unemployment, income inequality, extreme poverty, etc. The current Economic Ministry addressed that the economy will only return to its pre-crisis levels of December 2019 by 2022.

Constitutional Development of Nigeria

To understand good governance and realize the rights and liberty of people, the constitutional framework has always been played a very significant role. Nigeria's constitutional development can be categorized into two periods; pre-independence era, which covers six constitutional instruments (1914, 1922, 1946, 1951, 1954, and 1960) and the post-independence constitutional eras, encompassing three instruments (1963, 1979 and 1999). The pre-independence constitutional framework was enacted through an order-in-council of the British monarch, while later constitutions were enacted in two ways; an Act of parliament (1963 Constitution) and military decree (1979 and 1999).

Origin of the Nigerian Constitution

Nigeria was a colony of Britain immediately after the annexation of Lagos in 1861. The year 1906 marked significant in the history in Nigerian politics when the Lagos colonies were merged with the Niger coast territories of southern Nigeria. After that of the unification of the southern and northern territories in 1914 when the Colony and Protectorate of Southern Nigeria were merged with the Protectorate of Northern Nigeria and they were referred to as the Colony and protectorate of Nigeria. In place of a legislative council for the country, there was established an advisory body called the Nigerian council. The 1914 constitution was mere legislation for the Lagos colony with a council of 30 members of whom 17 were officials and 13 non-officials. But that did not have the real autonomy for real legislation; it was just an advisory council. The governor was not bound to comply with the advice. One of the important features of this constitution is – amalgamated the colony and protectorate of Southern Nigeria and Protectorate of Northern Nigeria, into a single colony.

1922 Constitution

In 1919, after assuming office, Sir Hugh Clifford, the governor, was stressed by the then West African congress, led by Caseley Hayford, to arrange for constitutions in West African subject states. This directed to the creation of the Clifford constitution of 1922. It led to the first electoral system in Nigeria and subsequently the first election was conducted into the legislative council. However, the election was centered on the limited franchise which restricted the election to those that earned a minimum of 100 pounds annually, which was very expensive for most Nigerians. It further announced a legislative council that substituted the Nigerian council. It comprised of 46 members with the governor as the head. However, the council could only legislate for the South. The governor legislated for the North via proclamation. There was also an executive council. It is noted that after Hugh Clifford, there were two other governors, Cameroon and Bernard Boudillion but they were unable to contribute much in terms of constitutional development. However, Boudilion divided Nigeria into East, West, and North for administrative purposes. This made the foundation for future regionalism. Thus, under this constitutional development, consolidated unification got momentum as with predominantly appointed Legislative Council for the whole country, but with jurisdiction largely in Southern Nigeria.

The Richard Constitution

Before, the end of 1944, the then governor, Sir Arthur Richards end of 1944 advocated for a new proposal for constitutional amendment. It was because from the pressures of educated elites for not representing the indigenous masses. The constitution provided for a new legislative council comprising of the governor, 16 official members, and 28 unofficial members. Of the 28, two were nominated by the governor while 4 were elected. The North had 11 members, the West had 8 members while the East had 6 members. The elected 4 were from Lagos and Calabar. It is noted that this constitution made the council legislate for the whole country. It also provided for regional houses of assembly. The members of the regional assembly were nominated by the native authority. However, they were only discussing national issues, but not legislative bodies. Moreover, it was from the house of assembly that members were nominated to the legislative council. It can be necessary to note that the constitution reduced the limited franchise from 100 pounds to 50 pounds. Despite this, one of the defects of this constitution was that it limited franchise to only Lagos and Calabar and the regional houses of assemblies could not make laws.

Macpherson Constitution

Due to the criticism of the Richard constitution, a new constitution was desired. The governor, Sir John Macpherson ascertain to include Nigerian in the constitutional making process. It supported the wide consultation of Nigerians even to the village levels. The constitution provided for a federal legislature called the house of representatives. It had 136 elected representatives, 6 ex-officio members, and 6 nominated by the governor. 68 members were from the North, 34 from the West, and 34 from the East. It also provided for regional legislatures that could make laws for their regions. The legislatures in the West and North were bi-cameral, each having a house of chiefs alongside the regional legislature. In the East, it was a unicameral legislature. It was also from the regional legislatures that members were nominated to the legislative council.

Lyttleton Constitution

Despite the developments in the Macpherson constitution, it was a failure to unite Nigerian. It dismissed soon due to problems from the legislature. In 1953, the question of granting independence arose. It creates several reactions and to settle the situations, the then colonial secretary, Oliver Lyttleton called the leaders for a conference in London. Several issues were consulted during the conference and committees were set up. Their reports were to be considered in the Lagos conference of 1954. The constitutional conferences of 1953 and 1954 held in London and Lagos respectively led to the creation of the Lyttleton constitution. The constitution fully introduced a federal system, with North, East, West, and Southern Cameroons. While the Federal capital territory was in Lagos. In judicial matters, the West African court of appeal was abolished. There was a supreme court for Nigeria and individual high courts for the regions. In the meantime, the Eastern and Western regions became self-governing in 1957 while the North became self-governing in 1959. Southern Cameroon through a referendum decided out of Nigeria.

The Independence Constitution

On 1st October 1960, after the independence of Nigeria, the Queen become the Governor-General (the Head of the state). The Prime minister was also appointed. Though this constitution was more like a 1954 constitution, some changes were taken place. It provided provisions for attaining citizenship of the Nigerians. The constitution allocated legislative powers between the center and the regional legislature. It contained provisions for the legislative list, concurrent list, and residual list that were legislated by central legislature, central & regional legislature and regional legislature respectively. It also made provisions for a dual executive -Head of State and the Head of Government are not the same. Moreover, there existed a constitutional supremacy for maintaining unity.

The 1963 Republican Constitution (First Republic)

This republican constitution came into effect on 1st October 1963. It established the country as a federal republic. One of the core features was that the queen of England terminated to be the head of state. The head of state was the president who was to be elected by secret ballot of a joint session of both houses of the national assembly. The Supreme court rather than the privy council became the highest court in the country. It is noted that the judicial Service commission was brought to an end and the appointment of judges bestowed in the prime minister. The power of judicial review was conferred in the Supreme Court. Moreover, the seats in the senate and house of representatives were greater than before. Despite all these changes in the constitution, there were several criticisms such as the president was elected by the national assembly instead of the electorates that consisted of just a few electorates, etc. Because of the rising political crises in the country, the republican constitution did not continue. However, on January 15, 1966, there was a military coup d'etat that overthrew the democratic institutions and accordingly took over by the military rule until 1979.

The Presidential Constitution of 1979(Second Republic)

In 1975, after coming to power General Murtala Muhammed assured to get back civilian rule to Nigeria. But due to his demise, this vision was put forward by Obasanjo.Sadly, he could not see this through as he was assassinated. Accordingly, a constituent assembly led by Justice Udo Udoma prepared a draft of the constitution and came into force on 1st, October 1979. Under this, the president was both head of state as well as the head of government, commander in chief of the armed forces. The president was elected by the electorates in a general election. But he did not have the power to appoint his ministers. There also prevailed an executive governor for each state who was the chief executive of the state. The legislature was made bicameral comprised of the senate(95 members) and the house of representatives (450 members), while the states had a unicameral legislature. The legislature endowed with the power of impeachment of the president while the house of assembly had the command to impeach the governor. Moreover, the judicial service commission was restored and had the powers to recommend judges for appointment subject to assent by the president and selected by the legislature. The judiciary had the ample power to interpret the constitution and can declare acts null and void if find unconstitutional.

1993 constitution (Third Republic)

The 1993 constitution was proposed to the reoccurrence of democratic rule to Nigeria with the establishment of a Third Republic. But unfortunately was never fully implemented, and the military resumed power until 1999.

1999 presidential constitution (Fourth Republic)

The 1999 constitution restored democratic rule to Nigeria and remains in force today. It emphasized different aspects of Nigerian laws and policies, talks about citizenship, the executive head, law systems, forms of elections, political parties. Section 38(1) of the 1999 constitution provides that every person shall be entitled to freedom of thought, conscience, and religion. In January 2011, two amendments to the 1999 constitution were signed by President Olusegun Obasanjo. Under this constitution, every person shall be entitled to his liberty and no person shall be deprived of such liberty. So this constitution helps to fulfill the aims and aspirations of the citizen of Nigeria.

In this way, various stages have passed by every country to attain the present day constitution and these constitutions have always been tried to protect the rights and liberties of every citizen.

Political Economy of Nigeria

Nigeria is a multi-ethnic and multi-culturally diverse federation which comprises of 36 autonomous states and the Federal Capital Territory. Nigeria's federated structure offers significant autonomy to states. The country returns to democracy in 1999. The last election was held in 2019 and Muhammadu Buhari became president for the second term in May 2019. He came to power with priority issues like combating corruption, tackling unemployment, boost the economy and living standards of people, etc. When we talk about the economy,

Nigeria is a mixed economy and ranked the 27th largest economy in the world in terms of nominal GDP. With plenty of natural resources, Nigeria is Africa's biggest oil exporter and has the largest reservoirs of natural gas of the continent. It is an emerging market with expanding manufacturing (in 2013 the manufacturing sector became largest in Africa), financial, service, communications, technology, and entertainment sectors. Moreover, the debt-to-GDP ratio is 16.075 percent as of 2019. Correspondingly, the GDP per capita doubled from $1400 per person in 2000 to an estimated $2,800 per person in 2012. Although Nigeria produces only about 2.7% of the world's oil supply. Although oil revenues contribute 2/3 of state revenues oil only contributes about 9% to the GDP. In the case of the agricultural sector, Nigeria once was a large net exporter of food but gradually it imports some of its food products.

Moreover, United Nations (UN) sponsored National Millennium Goals for Nigeria, a longer-term economic development program from 2000 to 2015, to attain a wide range of determined objectives involving poverty reduction, education, gender equality, health, the environment, and international development cooperation. It resulted in making progress but not sufficiently. Nigeria had made progressive efforts to provide universal primary education, protect the environment. Further, from 2003 to 2007, Nigeria endeavored to initiate an economic reform program called the National Economic Empowerment Development Strategy (NEEDS). The purpose of the NEEDS was to uplift the country's standard of living through a variety of reforms, including macroeconomic stability, deregulation, liberalization, privatization transparency, and accountability. It was basically to deal with basic areas like lack of freshwater and irrigation, insufficient power supply, poor infrastructure, corruption, unemployment, etc, and envisioned to create 7 million new jobs, improve non-energy sector exports, improve agricultural productivity, etc. Subsequently, the state level is the State Economic Empowerment Development Strategy (SEEDS) is also adopted.

In 2005, Nigeria agreed with the Paris Club of lending nations to remove all of its bilateral external debt. Under the agreement, the lenders will let off most of the debt, and Nigeria will pay off the remainder with a portion of its energy revenues. Since 2014, Nigeria's rapidly growing telecommunications, banking, and its film industry act as contributors to its GDP. But despite this, non-energy-related infrastructure is quite inadequate and in the case of human capital, it ranked as 152 out of a total of 157 countries in 2019.

Apart from this, the Nigerian economy suffers from an ongoing supply crisis in the power sector. Though since 2005, Nigerian power reforms have concentrated on encouraging private investment in the power sector. But a little increase in supply has been reported. It failed to provide adequate electricity supply to domestic households and industrial activities. Further, the Nigerian government faces challenges to protect the economy from oil price volatility. It is due to excessive dependence on oil that accounts for its revenues and foreign exchange earnings.

Points to Remember

- Magna Carta came to be the first historical charter which placed some limitations upon the exercise of powers by the king. It laid the foundations for the emergence of a limited monarchy in England.
- The Monarchy abolished between 1649-60. In this year, England continued to be a commonwealth under a written constitution.
- After the Chinese Civil War 1945-49 resulted in a decisive Communist victory. On October 1, 1949, Mao Zedong officially proclaimed the founding of the People's Republic of China.
- The Cultural Revolution that was initiated by Mao after the failure of the Great Leap Forward (1958), produced several big turmoils in the Chinese society and political system.
- The 1982 Constitution accepted Marxism-Leninism-Maoism but along with it, a new need for liberalization, decentralization, modernization and market socialism was accepted.
- Brazil had seven other constitutions over the yearsbeginning with the constitution of 1824

- Brazil is an emerging industrialized country with the largest share of global wealth in Latin America.It has a developing free-market economy, the 9th largest in the world in 2019.
- Nigeria's constitutional development can be categorized into two periods; pre-independence era, which covers six constitutional instruments (1914, 1922, 1946, 1951, 1954, and 1960) and the post-independence constitutional eras, encompassing three instruments (1963, 1979 and 1999).
- On 1st October 1960, after the independence of Nigeria, the Queen become the Governor-General (the Head of the state). The Prime minister was also appointed.The republican constitutio 1963 established Brazil as a federal republic. One of the core features was that the queen of England terminated to be the head of state.

Further Reading

J. McCormick, "*Comparative Politics in Transition*", (UK: Wadsworth, 2007), pp. 260-270.

L. Barrington, *"Comparative Politics - Structures & Choices",* (Boston: Wadsworth, 2010), pp. 212-13; 71-76; 84-89.

M. Grant, "*United Kingdom Parliamentary System' in The UK Parliament",* (Edinburgh:Edinburgh University Press, 2009), pp. 24-43.

M. Kesselman, J. Krieger and William, *"Introduction to Comparative Politics: Political Challenges and Changing Agendas,"* (UK: Wadsworth, 2010), pp. 47-70 (Britain); 364- 388 (Nigeria); 625-648 (China); 415-440 (Brazil).

Multiple Choice Questions

(a) In which year Magna Carta- the first historical charter that put limitations upon the exerciseof powers by the king established?

(i) 1215 (ii) 1512

(iii) 1425 (iv) 1856

(b) In which year Communist Party of China was founded ?

(i) 1921 (ii) 1934

(iii) 1922 (iv) 1919

(c) Cultural Revolution was initiated by whom?

(i) Mao Zedong (ii) Hitler

(iii) Gandhi (iv) Nelson Mandela

(d) In which year political conomy of China marked a move from a centrally planned system to a market-oriented economy.

(i) 1921 (ii) 1978

(iii) 1982 (iv) 1991

(e) In which year this first republican constitution was established in Brazil with a directly elected president.

(i) 1891 Constitution (ii) 1946 Constitution

(iii) 1967 Constitition (iv) 1969 Constitution

(f) In which year Peopl's Republic of China was established?

(i) 1921 (ii) 1949

(iii) 1982 (iv) 1947

(g) Which is the largest country in South America and Latin America ?

(i) Nigeria (ii) Brazil

(iii) China (iv) USA

(h) Nigeria was a colony of which country?

(i) Britain (ii) USA

(iii) France (iv) China

(i) Nigeria returns to democracy in which year?

(i) 1998 (ii) 1999

(iii) 1822 (iv) 2000

(j) Brazil is a type of country-

(i) Presidential Republic

(ii) Federal and Constitutional Republic

(iii) Communistiv. Constitutional Monarch

Notes

1. Carl Riskin, "*China's Political Economy*" (Oxford: Oxford University Press, 1987), p. 136.
2. "China's Economic Rise: History, Trends, Challenges, and Implications for the United States", *Congressional Research Service*, June, 2019.
3. Yang Yao, "The Political Economy causes of China's economic success".
4. Kate O'Keeffe, Michael C. Bender and Chun Han Wong, "Coronavirus Casts Deep Chill Over U.S.-China Relations: Pandemic has brought

relations between the two to a modern-day nadir as they try to outmaneuver one another to shape the world order", *Wall Street Journal*, May 6, 2020.

5. *Wong, Chun Han & Natasha, Khan "China Votes to Override Hong Kong's Autonomy on National Security: Resolution paves way for new legal and enforcement steps in Hong Kong to help China quash anti-Beijing protests, and sets up conflict with U.S." The Wall Street Journal, 28 May, 2020.*
6. Laura He, "China's economy may not grow at all in 2020. That hasn't happened in 44 years", *CNN Business*, 1April, 2020.
7. Luis Roberto Barroso, "Temas De Detairio Constitutional", (Rio De Janeiro, Renover, 2001), Vol. I, p. 10.

Bibliography

Abernethy, D. B. The Dynamics of Global Dominance: European Overseas Empires, 1415–1980. New Haven, CT: Yale University Press, 2000.

Acemoglu, D., S. Johnson, and J. Robinson. "The Colonial Origins of Comparative Development: An Empirical Investigation." American Economic Review 95, no. 5 (2000): 1369-1401.

Achebe, C. There Was a Country: A Personal History of Biafra. New York: Penguin Press, 2012. Amone, C., and O. Muura. "British Colonialism and the Creation of Acholi Ethnic Identity in Uganda, 1894 to 1962." The Journal of Imperial and Commonwealth History 42, no. 2 (2014): 239–257.

Andersen, L. "Outsiders Inside the State. Post-Conflict Liberia Between Trusteeship and Partnership." Journal of Intervention and Statebuilding 4, no. 2 (2010): 129–152.

Andreski, I. Old Wives' Tales: Life-Stories from Ibibioland. London: Routledge & K. Paul, 1970. Andrews, M., L. Pritchett, and M. Woolcock. Building State Capability. 1st ed. New York: Oxford University Press, 2017.

Bain, W. "For Love of Order and Abstract Nouns: International Administration and the Discourse of Ability." Journal of Intervention and Statebuilding 3, no. 2 (2009): 143–161.

Barbara, J. "Antipodean Statebuilding: The Regional Assistance Mission to Solomon Islands and Australian Intervention in the South Pacific." Journal of Intervention and Statebuilding 2, no. 2 (2008): 123–149.

Barnes, L. Africa in Eclipse. London: Gollancz, 1971. Bentley, T. Empires of Remorse: Narrative, Postcolonialism and Apologies for Colonial Atrocity. New York: Routledge, 2016.

Biber, B. Intertribal War in Pre-Colonial Namibia. Genève: Institut universitaire de hautes études internationales, 1989.

Bigman, L. History and Hunger in West Africa: Food Production and Entitlement in Guinea-Bissau and Cape Verde. Westport, CT: Greenwood Press, 1993.

Branch, D. "The Enemy within: Loyalists and the War against the Mau Mau in Kenya." Journal of African History 48, no. 2 (2007): 291–315.

Burns, A. S. Colonial Civil Servant. London: George Allen and Unwin, 1949. Burns, E. British Imperialism in West Africa. London: Labour Research Department, 1927.

Burton, A., and M. Jennings. "Introduction: The Emperor's New Clothes? Continuities in Governance in Late Colonial and Early Postcolonial East Africa." International Journal of African Historical Studies 40, no. 1 (2007): 1–25.

Cann, J. P. Counterinsurgency in Africa: The Portuguese Way of War, 1961–1974. Westport, CT: Greenwood Press, 1997.

Chandler, D. "The Uncritical Critique of 'Liberal Peace'." Review of International Studies 36, no. S1 (2010): 137–155.

Chatterjee Miller, M. Wronged by Empire. Stanford: Stanford University Press, 2013.

Chesterman, S. You, the People: The United Nations, Transitional Administration, and State-Building. Oxford: Oxford University Press, 2004.

Cohen, R. "The State in Africa." Review of African Political Economy 3, no. 5 (1976): 1–3.

Collier, P. Wars, Guns, and Votes: Democracy in Dangerous Places. 1st ed. New York: Harper, 2009. Cunliffe, P. "State-Building: Power without Responsibility." In State-Building: Theory and Practice, edited by A. Hehir and N. Robinson, 50–69. New York: Routledge, 2007.

Chilcote, Ronald H., Part I: Introduction, in Ronald H.Chilcote, Theories of Comparative Politics: The Search for a Paradigm Reconsidered, Westview Press, Boulder, 1994 (Second Edition).

Daniels, A. "Mau Mau Revisited." New Criterion June (2005): 21–26. Darwin, J. "Exit and Colonial Administrations." In Exit Strategies and State Building, edited by R. Caplan, 22–36. New York: Oxford University Press, 2012.

Landman, Todd, Issues and Methods in Comparative Politics: An Introduction, Routledge, London, 2000.

Mair, Peter, 'Comparative Politics: An Overview', in R.E.Goodin and H. Klingemann eds., The New Handbook of Political Science, Oxford University Press, Oxford; 1996.

Mohanty, Manoranjan, 'Comparative Political Theory and Third world Sensitivit', Teaching Politics, Nos. & 2, 1975.

Sartori, Giovanni, 'Compare, Why and How', in Mattei Dogan and Ali Kazancigil eds., Coyparing Nations, Concepts, Strategies, Substance, B lackwe l I, Oxford, 1994.

Wiarda, Roward J. 'Is Comparative Politics Dead? Rethinking the Field in the Post-Cold War Era', Third World Quarterly, Vol. 19, no.5. 646–663. doi:10.1093/afraf/adw030.

Grøner Krogstad, E. "Local Ownership as Dependence Management: Inviting the Coloniser Back." Journal of Intervention and Statebuilding 8, nos 2–3 (2014): 105–125.

Hammond, R. J. Portugal and Africa, 1815–1910: A Study in Uneconomic Imperialism. Stanford: Stanford University Press, 1966.

Hayward-Jones, J. Australia's Costly Investment in Solomon Islands: The Lessons of Ramsi. Canberra: Lowy Institute for International Policy, 2014.

Hechter, M. "Alien Rule and Its Discontents." American Behavioral Scientist 53, no. 3 (2009): 289–310.

Hechter, M. Alien Rule. Cambridge: Cambridge University Press, 2013.

Herbst, J. I. States and Power in Africa: Comparative Lessons in Authority and Control. Princeton, NJ: Princeton University Press, 2000.

Hönke, J. "Multinationals and Security Governance in the Community: Participation, Discipline and Indirect Rule." Journal of Intervention and Statebuilding 6, no. 1 (2012): 57–73.

Hopkins, A. G. The Future of the Imperial Past. Cambridge: Cambridge University Press, 1997. Houreld, K. "World Turns out to Hail Woman Who Carries Hopes of a Continent." The Times 29 (2006).

Ignatieff, M. "Nation-Building Lite." New York Times Magazine 151, no. 52193 (2002): 26.

Igreja, V. "Frelimo's Political Ruling through Violence and Memory in Postcolonial Mozambique." Journal of Southern African Studies 36, no. 4 (2010): 781–799.

Juan, A. D., and J. H. Pierskalla. "The Comparative Politics of Colonialism and Its Legacies: An Introduction." Politics & Society 45, no. 2 (2017): 159–172.

Kaplan, R. "In Defense of Empire." The Atlantic (2014). Lake, D. A., and C. J. Fariss. "Why International Trusteeship Fails: The Politics of External Authority in Areas of Limited Statehood." Governance 27, no. 4 (2014): 569–587.

Lange, M., J. Mahoney, and M. vom Hau. "Colonialism and Development: A Comparative Analysis of Spanish and British Colonies." American Journal of Sociology 111, no. 5 (2006): 1412–1462.

Lefebvre, C. "We Have Tailored Africa: French Colonialism and the 'Artificiality' of Africa's Borders in the Interwar Period." Journal of Historical Geography 37, no. 2 (2011): 191–202.

Lemay-Hébert, N. "Statebuilding without Nation-Building? Legitimacy, State Failure and the Limits of the Institutionalist Approach." Journal of Intervention and Statebuilding 3, no. 1 (2009): 21–45.Lemay-Hébert, N. "Critical Debates on Liberal Peacebuilding." Civil Wars 15, no. 2 (2013): 242–252. Levy, J. T., and I. M. Young. Colonialism and Its Legacies.

Lanham, MD: Lexington Books, 2011. Liebhold, D. "Businesses Brace for Return of Customs." Asian Business 33, no. 4 (1997): 12.

Lopes, C. Guinea-Bissau: From Liberation Struggle to Independent Statehood. London: Zed Books, 1987.

Lumumba, P. Congo, My Country. New York: Praeger, 1962.

Lüthi, Barbara, Francesca Falk, and Patricia Purtschert. "Colonialism without Colonies: Examining Blank Spaces in Colonial Studies." National Identities 18, no. 1 (2016): 1–9.

Matanock, A. "Governance Delegation Agreements: Shared Sovereignty as a Substitute for Limited Statehood." Governance 27, no. 4 (2014): 589–612.

Mayblin, L. Asylum after Empire: Colonial Legacies in the Politics of Asylum Seeking. New York: Roman & Littlefield International, 2017.

Mendy, P. K. "Amilcar Cabral and the Liberation of GuineaBissau: Context, Challenges and Lessons for Effective African Leadership." African Identities 4, no. 1 (2006): 7–21.

Midgley, J., and D. Piachaud. Colonialism and Welfare: Social Policy and the British Imperial Legacy. Cheltenham: Edward Elgar, 2011.

Miers, S., and M. A. Klein. Slavery and Colonial Rule in Africa. Portland, OR: Frank Cass, 1999.

Miles, W. F. S. Scars of Partition: Postcolonial Legacies in French and British Borderlands. Lincoln: University of Nebraska Press, 2014.

Misevich, P., and K. Mann. The Rise and Demise of Slavery and the Slave Trade in the Atlantic World. Rochester, NY: University of Rochester Press, 2016.

Mota, A. T. d. Guiné Portuguesa. 2 vols. Lisboa: Agência Geral do Ultramar, 1954.

Msiska, M.-H. "Imagined Nations and Imaginary Nigeria: Chinua Achebe's Quest for a Country." Journal of Genocide Research 16, no. 2–3 (2014): 401–419.

Murray, R. W., and A. Hehir. "Intervention in the Emerging Multipolar System: Why R2P Will Miss the Unipolar Moment." Journal of Intervention and Statebuilding 6, no. 4 (2012): 387–406.

Okafor, F. O. E. "The Paigc and the Economic Development of Guinea-Bissau: Ideology and Reality." The Developing Economies 26, no. 2 (1988): 125–140.

Olsson, Ola. "On the Democratic Legacy of Colonialism." Journal of Comparative Economics 37, no. 4 (2009): 534–551.

Plamenatz, J. On Alien Rule and Self-Government. London: Longmans, 1960.

Rabaka, R. Resistance and Decolonization, Reinventing Critical Theory. Lanham, MD: Rowman & Littlefield International, 2016.

Ribi Forclaz, A. Humanitarian Imperialism: The Politics of Anti-Slavery Activism, 1880–1940. Oxford: Oxford University Press, 2015.

Richmond, O. P., and J. Franks. Liberal Peace Transitions: Between Statebuilding and Peacebuilding. Edinburgh: Edinburgh University Press, 2009.

Riley, J. "The Timing and Pace of Health Transitions around the World." Population and Development Review 31, no. 4 (2005): 741–764.

Roberts, D. "Hybrid Polities and Indigenous Pluralities: Advanced Lessons in Statebuilding from Cambodia." Journal of Intervention and Statebuilding 2, no. 1 (2008): 63–86.

Romer, P. "Why the World Needs Charter Cities." 2009.

Sagar, R. "Are Charter Cities Legitimate?" Journal of Political Philosophy 24, no. 4 (2016): 509–529. Schofer, E., and A. Hironaka. "The Effects of World Society on Environmental Protection Outcomes." Social Forces 84, no. 1 (2005): 25–47.

Sèbe, B. "From Post-Colonialism to Cosmopolitan Nation-Building? British and French Imperial Heroes in Twenty-First-Century Africa." The Journal of Imperial and Commonwealth History 42, no. 5 (2014): 936–968.

Stanley, T. "History is Never Black and White." History Today 62, no. 12 (2012): 44.

Stilwell, S. "Constructing Colonial Power: Tradition, Legitimacy and Government in Kano, 1903-63." The Journal of Imperial and Commonwealth History 39, no. 2 (2011): 195–225.

Whalan, J. How Peace Operations Work: Power, Legitimacy, and Effectiveness. New York: Oxford University Press, 2014.

Williams, A. "The Postcolonial Flaneur and Other Fellow-Travellers: Conceits for a Narrative of Redemption." Third World Quarterly 18, no. 5 (1997): 821–842.

Wolfers, M. "West African Leader Seeks Talks with Portugal." The Times, 26 October 1971: 7. World Bank. Partnership for Capacity Building in Africa. Washington, DC: World Bank, Office of the Vice President, Africa Region, 1996.

Wu, T.-M. "A Re-Valuation of the Management of Dutch Taiwan." Taiwan Economic Review 44, no. 3 (2016): 379–412.

Young, C. The African Colonial State in Comparative Perspective. New Haven, CT: Yale University Press, 1994.

Young, C. "The Heritage of Colonialism." In Africa in World Politics: Constructing Political and Economic Order, edited by J. W. Harbeson and D. S. Rothchild, 9–26. Boulder, CO: Westview Press, 2016.

Ypi, L. E. A. "What's Wrong with Colonialism." Philosophy & Public Affairs 41, no. 2 (2013): 158–191.

Index

D

E

I

J

K

L

M

Z